THE TAILED AMPHIBIANS OF EUROPE

The European Salamander (*salamandra salamandra*)

The Tailed Amphibians of Europe

by J. W. STEWARD

DAVID & CHARLES : NEWTON ABBOT

Printed in Great Britain by
Latimer Trend & Company Limited Plymouth
for David & Charles (Publishers) Limited
Newton Abbot   Devon

Contents

List of Illustrations

DRAWINGS

PHOTOGRAPHS

The drawings are the work of the author. All photographs are by Grahame Dangerfield except Nos 1 and
2, which are published by courtesy of Dr P. V. Terentyev.

FIGURES

MAPS

Preface

THIS is the first published work dealing exclusively and in detail with the tailed amphibians of Europe, and as such, it is hoped that it will fill a long-standing gap. But time will undoubtedly show up its deficiencies as a pioneer work. While every effort has been made to check and re-check the factual information contained in it, the book is by no means intended to be of interest only to expert herpetologists. Rather than emphasise classifications and anatomical differences, these have been more or less limited to serving two purposes. One is to facilitate identification of the various species and sub-species; the other, and by far the more important, is to portray each form as a surviving result of a long period of continuous evolution, still capable of carrying out the many functions necessary for maintaining its existence. This is, after all, the main fascination of all forms of life, including our own, up to their point of extinction.

However, in order to write about the fauna of a given area, it is necessary first to classify that fauna, and this is by no means always so easy as the layman might think. The latest standard herpetological check-list for Europe is that published by Mertens and Wermuth in 1960, and their classification of the tailed amphibians has been adopted in its entirety in this book, though reservations are expressed in the text about the validity of a few subspecies. All check-lists are subject to change in the light of improved knowledge, and the list

11

given at the end of Chapter 2 (see p 39) of this book cannot be regarded as necessarily the last word on the subject. The ever-present question of what does, and what does not, constitute a species, not to mention the more arbitrary matter of a genus or a family, will no doubt continue to cause confusion from time to time, and although, for example, revision of the *Hydromantes* group in Europe has admirably simplified the position by lumping all five known forms into one species, so much still remains to be discovered about these secretive salamanders that further revision in due course seems almost inevitable. Apart from this, no zoologist, even a European one, is prepared altogether to give up the thought that hitherto undiscovered forms might be lurking somewhere in his terrain.

In illustrating the book, the choice was between photographs and drawings. Both have their advantages and disadvantages, but on balance it was decided to choose drawings reproduced by half-tone photography. Their main purpose is to aid identification, and drawings are more easily standardised for comparison and lend themselves better to emphasising diagnostic features than photographs. This may not please the purists, but is practicable. For species in which the males in particular develop skin appendages and brighter patterns during the breeding season, they are presented in this condition. A few photographs have been included for interest and mostly show the condition outside the breeding season.

In a work of this sort it would obviously be nonsensical to try to give the impression that all the information contained in it resulted from first-hand experience. I have carefully sifted all the available literature on the subject but have certainly not been able to check every fact personally. Nevertheless, the material for the book has taken years to collect, and while collecting it I have checked as much as possible. Most of the species and many of the subspecies have been studied first-hand in captivity or in the field. Further, much information has been obtained from unpublished material made available by the courtesy of other herpetologists. Finally, it has of course been necessary to decide what of all this mass of material from various sources should be accepted and what rejected. To this extent, I must accept responsibility for the accuracy or otherwise of the text.

CHAPTER 1

Evolutionary History of the Class Amphibia

THE amphibians were the first main type of vertebrate to adopt a widespread terrestrial habit, and correspondingly the first to develop a truly tetrapod form. The oldest known fossils of true amphibians have been found in late Devonian rocks in Greenland and Canada, together with remains of tropical plants indicating that at that time those areas enjoyed a warm, moist climate. One of these fossil forms is so close in many respects to the crossopterygian fish (Rensch, 1959) that the important step from fish to amphibian can hardly have taken place earlier than the middle of the Devonian period (Stirton, 1959). Both the plants and the invertebrates had preceded the vertebrates in colonising the land, so that food and shelter were plentiful, and during the late Devonian the amphibians spread and evolved very rapidly. This evolution continued throughout the Carboniferous, during which period some species reached quite a large size, and gave rise towards the end of the period to the first reptiles, which like-wise proceeded to diversify and in turn gave rise to the mammals and birds.

The later classes were in many ways physically superior to the amphibians, of which many orders died out to leave only three orders surviving at the present time, none of them in-cluding any really large species. The disadvantages from which the amphibians suffer in comparison with the later-evolving classes are considerable. The main disadvantage is that, unlike the reptiles, mammals and birds, the amphibians have never properly solved the problem of getting away from water. Not only are they still tied to a greater or lesser extent to moist surroundings, but, what is perhaps worse, it is with comparatively few exceptions necessary for them to return to the water to breed. It was by overcoming the close dependence on water that the later vertebrate forms opened up a new range of habitats. The basic requirements were twofold, affecting respectively respiration and reproduction, and in order to understand the limitations of the modern amphibians it is as well to examine the evolutionary history of these capacities. The crossopterygians were, of course, gill-breathing animals, but at some time during the Devonian a group of them developed a primitive form of lung which presumably enabled them, by swallowing air, to survive in oxygen-starved water and very probably during periods of drought, as do the three primitive species of lungfish which still exist. A further development was the modification of the pectoral and anal fins to form stalk-like appendages useful as an aid to locomotion in shallow, weedy waters, and it needs little stretch of the imagination to see how in one or more species these appendages could have been further modified and strengthened to become primitive legs, enabling their possessors to crawl from one pool to another as the pools dried up or food supplies ran short. From the crossopterygians arose two groups of particular subsequent importance. One converted the primitive lung into a swim-bladder, which opened the way to a pelagic existence in fresh and marine waters, while the other improved both lungs and legs so that the adult animals could take up a more or less terrestrial mode of life. The latter group became the amphibians, and by and large this is as far as many of them have ever got. They still largely depend on the skin as well as the lungs for

Page 17   Spotted Salamander *Salamandra s. salamandra*
          Alpine Salamander *Salamandra atra*

Page 18   Siberian Salamander *Hynobius keyserlingi*
                Gold-striped Salamander *Chioglossa lusitanica*
                Pyrenean Mountain Salamander *Euproctus asper*
                Sardinian Mountain Salamander *Euproctus platycephalus*

respiration, and this is the main reason why moist habitats are still generally necessary for them. Some have even regressed in the sense that the lungs have disappeared and respiration takes place through the skin and a specially-developed vascular lining of the mouth and throat.

Such evidence as is available from the fossil record indicates that the young of some at least of the earliest amphibians were entirely aquatic, furnished with external gills for respiration in water, and it is likely that this was the normal development of the amphibians in their early stages. It is certainly true that most existing species go through this form of development, whereby the young are aquatic and achieve much of their growth before the lungs develop and the animal can leave the water. In a few cases, as will be mentioned later, the eggs are laid on land and hatch out in the adult form, thus doing away with the aquatic larval stage, and one of the European species (*Salamandra atra*) has even gone so far as to suppress both the external egg and larval stages and produce living young on land.

Let us now consider the three main groups of amphibians which have survived to the present day. The group which has changed least from the original form is that of the tailed amphibians or urodeles (Order *Caudata* or *Urodela*). With few exceptions they are born of eggs laid in water, pass through an aquatic larval stage during which respiration is by external gills and the legs develop, until finally the gills atrophy, the lungs complete their development, and the animal leaves the water to take up life on land. This usually involves a breeding season, when the adults return to the water to lay their eggs. In some cases the eggs are fertilised direct by the male, but more usually fertilisation is internal by means of a spermatophore which is deposited by the male and picked up by the female after a more or less elaborate courtship display. An excellent review of courtship patterns in the urodeles is given by Salthe (1967). There are many exceptions

B

to this generalised life-history. Some genera and species are permanently aquatic and retain the gills throughout life. Others are permanently terrestrial and the eggs are laid on land, hatching in the adult form. Among the European species, *Salamandra salamandra* is viviparous, the young being deposited in water in the larval stage, and in *Salamandra atra* the young are born alive on land in the adult form.

The second main group is that of the frogs and toads, or anurans (Order *Salientia* or *Anura*). The members of this group mostly go through the same steps in developing from eggs laid in water through an aquatic larval stage into tetrapod land animals, but invariably the tail is absorbed at about the time that the tadpole leaves the water and the limbs are more or less adapted for active locomotion by walking or jumping. Here again there are exceptions to the general rule. The toads are by and large poor jumpers and prefer to walk or run. Many of them are excellent burrowers and most have fairly thick, warty skins which enable them to withstand much drier conditions than can most other amphibians, but even so a store of water has to be maintained from which the animal can keep the skin to some degree moist to facilitate skin respiration and avoid desiccation. Many exceptions are also met with in reproduction. Some frogs lay their eggs on land or in trees and bushes, sometimes in elaborate froth nests formed from secretions whipped up by the legs; the eggs hatch out in these nests and either the tadpoles complete their development there or the nests are made overhanging water into which the tadpoles fall. A good many anurans even practise protective behaviour towards their eggs or young. In the European Midwife Toad (*Alytes obstetricans*) the male wraps the eggs around his hind legs and carries them about for some time, even taking care to moisten them at intervals, and releases the larvae in water when they hatch out. The male of the aquatic Surinam Toad (*Pipa pipa*) spreads the eggs on the back of the female, into which they sink and from which the young eventually emerge in the adult form. The female of the Marsupial Frog (*Gastrotheca marsupiatum*) of South America has a dorsal pouch into which the eggs are placed by the male as they are fertilised, and the tadpoles, on reaching a certain size, are liberated by the female into water. In almost all the anurans fertilisation is external and takes place when the eggs are laid, to facilitate which the male at this time seizes and may be carried about by the female in what is known as 'amplexus'. In some exceptional cases fertilisation is internal, as with the so-called 'Tailed Frogs' of the genus *Ascaphus* from North America, in which the 'tail' of the male constitutes an intromittent organ for this purpose. Of a few species, such as *Rhacophorus microtympanum* of Ceylon, it has been reported that the aquatic larval stage has been completely dispensed with and the eggs are laid and hatch in moist soil or moss, the young emerging as perfectly formed froglets (Kirtisinghe, 1957).

The third group, the Caecilians, is in many respects retrograde, at least as far as the bodily form is concerned. This is a group which has taken to burrowing and in which as a result, as in the various snake and lizard groups which have adopted a similar existence, many physical changes have taken place, including the virtual disappearance of certain organs not needed in a subterranean habitat. The body has become considerably elongated, the legs have disappeared, and the eyes have become either functionless or nearly so. On the other hand, the aquatic larval stage has in most cases been suppressed and the eggs are laid and hatch out in underground chambers. Moreover, parental care of the eggs seems to have been more widely developed in this group than in any other, for in some species at least the female remains with the eggs, coiled around them, until they hatch.

The distribution of the three groups is interesting from many points of view. The anurans are practically worldwide, being found throughout most of Asia, Europe, Africa and Madagascar, North and South America, Australia and even New Zealand, as well as much of the general Indonesian area and many of the Pacific islands. The caecilians are restricted to tropical areas in a belt extending across South America, Asia, Africa, and the Seychelles. The urodeles are confined almost entirely to the Northern hemisphere, occurring throughout Asia, Europe, and North America, almost up to the Arctic circle, but absent from Australasia and the Pacific islands except for some adjoining the Asiatic mainland (such as the Ryu-kyus), and not found in Africa south of the Sahara. In the New World some genera extend into Central and South America, presumably having arrived in the latter area comparatively recently. In general, the urodeles are mainly found in areas of temperate climate and their original home may well have been in Asia, though some important evolutionary steps have obviously taken place in the New World.

Before examining the distribution of the urodeles in Europe, it may be helpful to elaborate a little on the various groups represented there and how these are distributed in various parts of the world. One family prominently represented in Europe is the *Salamandridae*, divided into various genera all with much in common. The main genus in Europe is *Triturus*, the members of which are commonly known as 'newts'; it embraces in all about a dozen species, of which eight are found in Europe and the remainder in southeast Asia and north-west Africa. Other closely related genera are found further afield, as for example *Cynops* in East Asia, and *Notophthalmus* and *Taricha* in North America. *Notophthalmus* is so closely related to *Triturus* that for a long time it was included in the same genus, and it is of interest in tracing the evolution of these newts that certain fossil specimens from western Europe seem to be identical with *Notophthalmus*. In the same way, *Cynops* was at one time lumped together with *Triturus*. All these newts are similar in general appearance and in their life-histories. All resort to water to lay their eggs, which hatch out as tadpoles with external gills; the tadpoles subsequently grow legs, develop lungs, and leave the water as smaller editions of the adults. All have a more or less elaborate courtship procedure, as will be described in greater detail for the European species. Other genera of the *Salamandridae* are mostly known as 'salamanders', of which there are some species in Europe and quite a number in North America.

Another family represented in Europe is the *Plethodontidae*, or lungless salamanders. True, this representation consists of only one species with a fairly limited distribution in South Europe, but in the New World the plethodontids are considerably more widespread and divergent, with a wide range of habitat.

The *Cryptobranchidae*, which retain their gills throughout life and are permanently aquatic, are represented by genera in East Asia and North America. They are large, the Asian genus *Megalobatrachus* including the largest living tailed amphibians.

Another persistently aquatic group is the family *Proteidae*, limited to a few species in South Europe and North America. In the adult stage at least they are mostly cave-dwellers, with rudimentary eyes, elongated bodies and permanent gills.

The families represented in Europe will be dealt with in greater detail in subsequent chapters, but it will be seen from the above brief outline that there is a strong connection between families in the Old and the New Worlds. The latest connection in geological time between the two areas was by means of a bridge over what is now the Bering Strait, and this fairly readily explains the distribution of the *Cryptobranchidae*, but it is rather surprising that some other groups are more or less confined to Europe and America. This is particularly evident in the newts, in which for example *Notophthalmus* and *Triturus* are more closely related to each other than to any of the Asian genera. Also the *Proteidae* and the plethodontid genus *Hydromantes* are represented outside America only by European populations which are very limited in their distribution and appear to be relict populations left behind in particularly suitable or sheltered habitats. A probable explanation is that this is a result of the periods of glaciation which occurred in the Northern hemisphere, and a fuller account of the presumed effects of these will be given in Chapter 2. Unfortunately, the fossil record is of very little help in following the movements which gave rise to the present distribution, and it is difficult to find a really satisfactory answer to such problems as the absence of the above-mentioned forms from Asia or of the tailed amphibians in general from Africa south of the Sahara and from Australasia. The only general pattern which seems to emerge is that when they first arose the urodeles were adapted to a temperate climate, that their main development took place in the Northern hemisphere, and that only a few specialised genera such as *Bolitoglossa* developed the necessary adaptations for life in tropical forests (including the ability to adopt an arboreal existence) and were thereby enabled to extend their range across the equator. The timing of this development was presumably such that this step was possible only in the New World, and elsewhere seas and deserts proved effective barriers. Therefore, in the Old World, the urodeles have everywhere been limited to the belt bordered by permafrost in the north and seas and deserts in the south, and since the recurrent periods of glaciation must have compressed the north-to-south width of this belt quite considerably from time to time, it is easier to understand why the existing families and genera occupy such disjointed ranges and include so many obviously relict populations. It is also obvious that the most widely spread families and genera are those which include species capable of withstanding severe winter conditions, either by pronounced tolerance for cold or to a much lesser extent by adaptation to life in underground waters.

Taking all the factors already mentioned into account—the existing distribution of the urodeles, the flimsy evidence of the fossil record, and the known climatic and geographical changes during the last million years or so—a general pattern emerges for which a number of tentative deductions regarding the ancestry of the present-day urodeles can be made.

Undoubtedly one of the key factors in explaining the present distribution is the series of periods of glaciation (popularly referred to as the 'Ice Ages') which lasted altogether about a million years (Wooldridge & Morgan, 1959) in the Northern hemisphere, and from the last of which large areas of Europe, Asia, and North America have barely emerged. There is, however, a big difference in the effects of these glaciations on the urodele populations of Europe and Asia on the one hand, and North America on the other. As regards the former, owing to the seas, deserts, and to some extent the mountain barriers generally bordering the southern edge of Eurasia, the incursion of the ice from the north greatly compressed the north-to-south width of the area in which the urodeles, in common with many other forms of life, were able to continue in existence. Moreover, inside this overall area separate ice-caps which formed in elevated areas such as the Alps and the Carpathians spread at times to such an extent that they tended to divide the narrow east-to-west strip of ice-free territory into segments. With each separate glaciation, therefore, the urodeles of Asia and particularly of Europe were confined in a number of comparatively small refuges, whole areas of population being wiped out in the process, and in the intervening interglacial periods the surviving remnants of the original populations slowly spread out again to occupy the once more ice-free territories, only to be decimated anew with the next encroachment of the ice. This helps to explain the existence of so many relict populations, and the wide gaps between similar forms in different continents.

In North America, similar incursions of ice from the north took place, but taking the area of North America as a whole the resulting devastation affected only the northern part of the area and a large expanse in the south was comparatively little affected. It is noticeable that, moving south to north in North America, the number of existing species of reptiles and amphibians decreases suddenly as the formerly glaciated areas are reached and in those areas, with very few exceptions, the species represented still have their roots, as it were, in the areas which remained free from glaciation.

In Asia, although a few hardy species have extended north into Siberia and west as far as the Urals, the tailed amphibians are largely based on the south-east corner of the continent, including the more adjacent islands such as Japan, Taiwan and the Ryu-kyus. Further west in Asia the urodeles are generally absent from the southern fringes of the continent and the off-lying islands. In Ceylon, for example, where Kirtisinghe (1957) listed over thirty species of amphibians, the only tailed amphibians included were two closely related species of caecilian, while the urodeles were not represented.

The following list of families illustrates the at first sight somewhat erratic distribution of the urodeles:

Amphiumidae. One species only in south-east North America.
Plethodontidae. Over 50 species covering most of temperate North America, with a much smaller number of species in Central and South America, and represented in Europe only by a few relict populations in the extreme south.
Salamandridae. The most widespread of all the families, covering most of the temperate zone in the Northern hemisphere, including North America, Europe, North Africa, the Asiatic mainland, Japan, and other islands off south-east Asia.

Ambystomidae. Widespread in North America from Canada to Mexico.

Cryptobranchidae. Two genera only, one in the east of North America and the other in China and Japan.

Hynobiidae. Some two dozen or so species, mostly in Japan and south-east Asia, but covering temperate Asia generally as far west as the Urals and north to the edge of the Arctic. One species (*Hynobius keyserlingi*) will be included in this book as forming part of the European fauna, but gains this position more or less on a technicality, as only a minute portion of its extensive range from the Urals to Kamchatka falls within European Russia.

Proteidae. Two genera only, one in North America and the other in southern Europe.

Sirenidae. Two genera in the south-east of North America.

To summarise, of the eight families comprising the urodeles, two are split between the New World and Europe, one is split between the New World and Asia, one is found in all three continents, three are confined to the New World, and one is virtually confined to Asia. Odd though this apparent irregularity of distribution may be at first sight, a few minutes' study of a map of the world will show how it could have arisen if we assume for each family a suitable point of origin in the Northern hemisphere and allow for greater or lesser extension of the range (according to the age of the family) during periods of mild climate, followed by the need to yield ground in the north during harsher climatic conditions.

Chapter 2 will explain in greater detail the effect of this on the tailed amphibian populations of Europe.

General Survey of the European Tailed Amphibians

IN Europe more than anywhere else in the world the distribution of cold-blooded animals bears the imprint of the geologically recent ice ages, referred to in Chapter 1. Their effect will be dealt with in greater detail in this chapter, not only because it goes a long way towards explaining the present distribution of the tailed amphibians in Europe, but also because it was presumably a major factor in bringing about the considerable diversification into subspecies which some of the species show.

It is, of course, not possible to consider in detail the separate effect of each of the series of ice ages, since we have little to guide us in trying to guess what urodele populations were living in Europe between any two of them. In fact, if we concentrate on the probable effect of the last period of glaciation, we have probably gone as far as we can in deciding the cumulative effect of all of them, since the difference can largely be only a question of degree. What is certain is that at least four times during the last million years (Wooldridge & Morgan, 1959) the climatic conditions in Europe were such that the whole urodele population must have been exterminated except in a few limited refuges. It is obviously important to consider what could have been the nature of these refuges, in conjunction with the habits of the species which might have taken advantage of them. For this purpose, it is convenient to divide the existing urodeles of Europe into three groups:

1. Those which are generally adapted to life in temperate forests.
2. Mountain forms capable of living in cold conditions at high altitude.
3. Subterranean forms.

Most species belong to Group 1, the more notable exceptions being:

Group 2—*Euproctus, Salamandra atra, Triturus montandoni*, and to some extent *T. alpestris*.

Group 3—*Hydromantes* and *Proteus*.

Before going on to consider each of these groups separately, let us try to imagine the probable effects on habitat of the climatic changes which accompanied the ice ages. There is no doubt that during each interglacial the climate was such that temperate forests were able to spread over most of Europe south of the existing tundra line and outside the high mountain ranges. As each ice age developed, the ice spread down from the north to cover most of the British Isles, Scandinavia, the northern parts of Germany, and much of Poland. In addition, glaciers radiated out from the higher mountain masses further south—the Alps, the Pyrenees, and the Carpathians. Even outside the actual areas of glaciation, the rest of Europe became so cold that the deciduous forests were wiped out almost everywhere except along the southern fringes, where the proximity of the Mediterranean probably had an ameliorating effect on climate. The successive ice ages were not all of equal intensity, but the overall effect on the fauna and flora probably varied less than the extent of the incursion of the ice. Fig 1 shows the approximate maximum extension of ice over the whole of the period, and indicates roughly the areas bordering the Mediterranean where temperate forests, and presumably therefore the more hardy urodeles, were able to survive. The intervening areas between the ice and the forests were, as far as can be judged by loess deposits and other geological indications, for a period mostly bare of forests and more or less the equivalent of tundra.

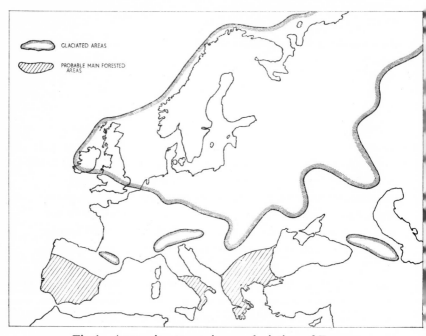

GLACIATED AREAS

PROBABLE MAIN FORESTED AREAS

Fig 1   Approximate maximum glaciation of Europe
during the Ice Ages

As will be seen from Fig 1, the forests at the height of the period of maximum glaciation were largely limited to two main areas in the south-west and south-east of Europe respectively, the former in the Iberian Peninsula and the latter to the west and south of the Black Sea, including also possibly an area immediately to the north of the Black Sea. A third minor area of forest probably survived along much of the coastal strip bordering the Mediterranean between the two main areas, and a fairly large area in Italy may well have retained a reasonably temperate climate. There is, however, a very good reason why this minor refuge was of less importance than the others. Owing to the amount of water locked up in the Polar ice-cap at its time of greatest expansion, the levels of the sea were for a time well below what they are today, so that the British Isles were connected to the Continent, Spain was almost certainly for a time joined to the north-west corner of Africa, the Black Sea was reduced in area and much of the area occupied by the Greek islands must have been above water. On the other hand, although Sicily may well have been joined to Italy for a while, and it is possible that Sardinia and Corsica were likewise joined to the European mainland, the depth of the sea between the African coast and Sicily and Sardinia respectively is such that this channel probably remained open throughout most if not all the series of glaciations. The general effect of all this was that the south-west refuge was open for a period to Africa in the south, and the south-east refuge was not only open into Asia Minor but undoubtedly covered a much larger area than is contained within the present coastal boundaries. The central refuge, on the other hand, in addition to being smaller than the others, was limited north and south by ice and sea respectively and completely isolated, except to the extent that a decrease in size of the Adriatic might for a time have opened up a connection with the Balkans.

Group 1

With the advance of the ice, the urodeles inhabiting the temperate forests of Europe must have been largely or entirely wiped out north of a line drawn roughly through the Pyrenees, the Alps, and the Carpathians. This left virtually only the three refuges—the two main ones to the south-west and the south-east and the smaller central one—in which remnants of the original European populations could have survived. It is likely that the populations in these respective refuges already differed somewhat and that even species common to more than one were differentiated genetically, especially where they were the peripheral elements of widely ranging species. The comparatively small size and limited gene pool of each remnant population, as well as the change in climatic conditions necessitating rapid adaptation, would tend to induce further evolutionary changes and enhance the existing differences even more than might have resulted from normal genetic drift. Following the recession of the ice, one of three things could happen to each of the forms in a given refuge:

1. It would spread slowly north again, in some cases eventually joining up in Central Europe with races from one or more of the other refuges, thus giving rise to further subspecies by hybridisation or creating areas of intergradation. This seems to have happened, for example, with *S. salamandra* during the period following the last glaciation.

2. It would fail to adapt itself in time to changing climatic conditions in the refuge, and die out.

3. It would fail to spread but succeed in adapting itself to changing conditions and remain in the refuge as a local species or subspecies. This would seem to have happened with *Chioglossa*, now confined to north-west Spain and Portugal; *Pleurodeles waltl*, found only in the south and south-west of the Iberian Peninsula and in Morocco; and *Salamandrina*, which is restricted to parts of the Italian peninsula. It must be appreciated that the Pyrenees and the Alps were in any case difficult barriers to cross by those populations which spread back into Central Europe from the south-west and central refuges, and it is no wonder that not all managed to achieve this.

The whole process must have taken place in its entirety at

least four times quite recently (geologically speaking), and while it is difficult to assess the effects of some of the minor cold periods which occurred during the main interglacials, these also must have resulted in similar changes, even if to a lesser degree. There can be no doubt that the total longer-term effect of all this must have been to speed up the rate of evolution of the species in this group quite considerably, and without going into details, it can be said that a comparison of the urodele populations of Europe and other parts of the world supports the view that in Europe such an acceleration has taken place.

Group 2
There are two types of urodele which come under this heading:

1. Those which can live only under cool conditions normally found at high elevations in temperate climates.
2. Those which are sufficiently adaptable to be able to withstand lower temperatures, but can also live in a normal temperate climate.

The species comprising the first type would obviously have been confined to elevated areas during the interglacials and would either have failed to survive the glacial periods or would have hung on in small pockets in sufficiently favourable locations in or near their original range. A further glance at Fig 1 will show that the most likely places for this would be along the southern edges of the main mountain ranges, particularly the Pyrenees and the Alps, where the proximity of the Mediterranean (even if reduced in area) would have had an ameliorating effect on the local climate. It is therefore perhaps understandable that the typical mountain species of Europe are found in the general area of the Alps and the Pyrenees. *Salamandra atra* is confined to the Alps proper and the mountainous regions along the east coast of the Adriatic, while the three species of *Euproctus* are found respectively in the Pyrenees and the mountains of Corsica and Sardinia.

The best example of the second type is the Alpine Newt, *Triturus alpestris*, which is at home at both high and low elevations. One can well imagine that such an adaptable species was widespread in north and central Europe during the last interglacial period and was reduced to a series of small colonies along the southern fringe of Europe during the final glaciation. The present distribution of the seven subspecies of this newt indicates that only one was able to extend subsequently into central Europe, and that the other six remained more or less *in situ* in south Europe.

Triturus montandoni, now found high in and around the Carpathians, is rather an anomaly in being the only European species proper entirely separated from the Mediterranean fringe. It is possible that it survived the last ice age in the Danube basin.

Group 3

Two families are represented in this group in Europe, the *Proteidae* and the *Plethodontidae*. In each case the family is more widespread in the New World and represented in Europe by only one species, although in the plethodontid species several subspecies are recognised which until fairly recently were regarded as constituting separate species. Each species is confined to a fairly limited area in south Europe, and in fact the two areas are only narrowly separated from each other. They can be regarded as truly relict populations in Europe of the families to which they belong, since these must at one time have had a wider distribution in Europe and Asia as well as the New World. In other words, they have died out at some time in Asia and most of Europe, and it is probable that the ice ages had a lot to do with this. The fact that one species from each family was able to survive in south Europe may in part be due to both species being basically subterranean in habit. The

Page 35 Iberian Ribbed Newt *Pleurodeles waltl*
Alpine Newt *Triturus alpestris* (male)
Alpine Newt *Triturus alpestris* (female)
Cave Salamander *Hydromantes genei*

Page 36   Northern Crested Newt *Triturus c. cristatus* (male)
             Northern Crested Newt *Triturus c. cristatus* (female)
             Alpine Crested Newt *T. cristatus carnifex* (male)
             Alpine Crested Newt *T. cristatus carnifex* (female)

proteid species, *Proteus anguinus*, is not only subterranean but entirely aquatic in underground lakes and streams in the limestone areas along the eastern borders of the Adriatic; the plethodontid species, *Hydromantes genei*, inhabits the northern part of Italy, overlapping into the extreme south-east of France as well as Sardinia, and spends most of its time underground in fissured limestone areas. The adaptations to their habitats of these two species will be discussed in greater detail in later chapters, but there can be little doubt that the ability to live underground played a large part in enabling them to survive the ice ages, in an area where the climate must have been at times very cold, but which was outside the main areas of glaciation and permafrost. The protection afforded against extremes of temperature even in shallow caves is quite remarkable. As examples, the temperature inside Kent's Cavern at Torquay in Devon, not a deep cave as caves go, rarely varies more than a few degrees either side of 53° F, winter and summer, and in the large cave system at Postojna in northern Yugoslavia where *Proteus* occurs, the air temperature remains constant between 47° and 48° F.

On the basis of the three groups postulated above, a simple survey of the European tailed amphibians can be drawn up. The bulk of the existing species belongs to the *Salamandridae*, and most of these are basically forest-dwellers which retreated with the forests during the glacial periods to become more or less confined to the southern refuges (with some species split over more than one refuge) and spread out again with the forests as the ice receded. The existing species with extensive ranges and considerable diversification into subspecies all belong to this family, as do several species with little or no diversification left behind in one or other of the refuges. A few species adapted to elevated habitats survived but remained restricted to a fairly limited range in each case, the only exception to this being *Triturus alpestris*, which although adapted to high altitudes is certainly not limited to them. Any other

c

families which might have been represented in Europe before the ice ages were wiped out there, except for small relict populations of the *Proteidae* and the *Plethodontidae*, limited to one species apiece, which managed to hang on in the south, presumably helped in this by their adaptation to an underground existence. The remaining family, the *Hynobiidae*, can claim to be represented in Europe only because one Asian species has crept over the border into European Russia, undoubtedly as part of an extension of its range following the last retreat of the ice.

It is obvious that those species which broke out of the refuges after the last period of glaciation did not all spread at the same rate, and this is illustrated as much as anything by the unique position of the British Isles. For quite some time after the last retreat of the ice was well under way, England was still joined to the Continent by a broad belt of land covering what is now the eastern end of the English Channel and the southern part of the North Sea. A good deal of research and speculation has gone into the question of how long ago it was that the English Channel was finally breached, and the general opinion at present is that this probably took place between 7,000 and 6,000 BC (Zeuner, 1958). This obviously suggests that the three species native to the British Isles, *Triturus cristatus, vulgaris* and *helveticus*, reached the area of the British Channel before the sea broke through, but the other species whose range is now bounded by the English Channel— *T. alpestris* and *S. salamandra*—arrived at a later date. Within the confines of the British Isles, Ireland was connected to south-west Scotland up to a date which is by no means certain, but which was very probably a good deal earlier than the separation of England from the Continent. It is therefore of interest that only one species, *T. vulgaris*, succeeded in colonising Ireland, and this is the species which elsewhere in Europe has penetrated the furthest north.

LIST OF THE EUROPEAN TAILED AMPHIBIANS

Family *Hynobiidae*	
Hynobius keyserlingi	Siberian Salamander
Family *Salamandridae*	
Salamandra salamandra	European Salamander
S. s. salamandra	Spotted Salamander
S. s. almanzoris	Central Spanish Fire Salamander
S. s. bejarae	Spanish Fire Salamander
S. s. corsica	Corsican Fire Salamander
S. s. fastuosa	Pyrenean Fire Salamander
S. s. gallaica	Portuguese Fire Salamander
S. s. gigliolii	Italian Fire Salamander
S. s. terrestris	Banded Salamander
Salamandra atra	Alpine Salamander
Chioglossa lusitanica	Gold-striped Salamander
Euproctus asper	Pyrenean Mountain Salamander
E. a. asper	
E. a. castelmouliensis	
Euproctus montanus	Corsican Mountain Salamander
Euproctus platycephalus	Sardinian Mountain Salamander
Pleurodeles waltl	Iberian Ribbed Newt
Salamandrina terdigitata	Spectacled Salamander
Triturus alpestris	Alpine Newt
T. a. alpestris	Alpine Newt
T. a. apuanus	Italian Alpine Newt
T. a. cyreni	Spanish Alpine Newt
T. a. lacusnigri	Balkan Alpine Newt
T. a. montenigrus	Montenegran Alpine Newt
T. a. reiseri	Bosnian Alpine Newt
T. a. veluchiensis	Greek Alpine Newt
Triturus boscai	Bosca's Newt

Triturus cristatus	Crested Newt
T. c. cristatus	Northern Crested Newt
T. c. carnifex	Alpine Crested Newt
T. c. dobrogicus	Danube Crested Newt
T. c. karelinii	Southern Crested Newt
Triturus helveticus	Palmate Newt
T. h. helveticus	Palmate Newt
T. h. sequeirai	Iberian Palmate Newt
Triturus marmoratus	Marbled Newt
T. m. marmoratus	Marbled Newt
T. m. pygmaeus	Southern Marbled Newt
Triturus montandoni	Carpathian Newt
Triturus vittatus	Banded Newt
T. v. ophryticus	Banded Newt
Triturus vulgaris	Smooth Newt
T. v. vulgaris	Smooth Newt
T. v. ampelensis	Rumanian Smooth Newt
T. v. borealis	North Swedish Smooth Newt
T. v. dalmaticus	Dalmatian Smooth Newt
T. v. graecus	Greek Smooth Newt
T. v. italicus	South Italian Smooth Newt
T. v. lantzi	Caucasian Smooth Newt
T. v. meridionalis	Southern Smooth Newt
T. v. schreiberi	Schreiber's Smooth Newt
Family *Plethodontidae*	
Hydromantes genei	Cave Salamander
H. g. genei	Sardinian Cave Salamander
H. g. ambrosii	Spezia Cave Salamander
H. g. gormani	Central Cave Salamander
H. g. italicus	Eastern Cave Salamander
H. g. strinatii	Western Cave Salamander
Family *Proteidae*	
Proteus anguinus	Olm

CHAPTER 3

The Family Hynobiidae

TAKE a map of Asia, cut off the strip north of the Arctic Circle and the tropical area south of the Himalayas, and what is left is roughly the area covered by the family *Hynobiidae*. Most of its two dozen or so species, divided into several genera, are found in Japan and continental East Asia, but members of the family are distributed from the Urals to the Pacific and from the Arctic south to the mountains of south-west Asia and South China, as well as on Taiwan, Japan, Sakhalin Island, and the Kuriles.

Their form is typical of that of most salamanders, and they are generally small in size, few exceeding a total length of 6 in and most being even shorter. A series of vertical (costal) grooves is present along each flank. Both jaws bear teeth and two rows of teeth are also present in the roof of the mouth in two wavy rows, converging posteriorly on the palate in most cases. The adults in most species are normally terrestrial but resort to water during the breeding season. In all of them fertilisation is external and takes place in water. The eggs hatch out into aquatic larvae furnished with external gills which eventually disappear to be replaced by lungs, except in one or two lungless species in which respiration takes place through the skin and by means of a vascularised membrane in the mouth and throat. The metamorphosed larvae leave the water when the gills disappear and live on land until they return to water again for breeding, with the exception of some specialised species which live a more or less aquatic life.

41

The only genus which concerns us here is *Hynobius*, which has a range extending over most of that covered by the family, its various species being found from the Urals to the Pacific and from the edge of the Arctic south to Turkestan, South China, Taiwan, and Japan.

Loveridge (1946) and Thorn (1962: 1963: 1967) have described the breeding procedure of a typical member of the genus, *Hynobius nebulosus*. In early spring the males and soon afterwards the females emerge from hibernation and make their way to the water, eventually assembling into groups, the members of which start swimming to and fro and up and down in the water for a period of some hours at a time. Following this period of apparent courtship behaviour, each female deposits two spindle-shaped gelatinous bags, attaching them to a rock, water-plants and the like, each bag being about 6 in long (after having increased in size through absorption of water) and containing some 35 to 70 eggs. The males then swim slowly to and fro over the bags (Loveridge) or actually seize them (Thorn) in order to fertilise them. The eggs hatch out in due course into larvae about $\frac{1}{2}$ in long, which emerge from the bag and commence to swim freely. For the first two or three weeks they feed on vegetable slime and possibly infusoria, and later on small water creatures such as insect larvae, fish-fry, and tadpoles. When the gills finally atrophy and the young salamanders leave the water they adopt the secretive life of the adults on land, spending the day under cover in damp places and coming out at night to feed on insects, grubs, worms, and the like.

Only one species of the genus, *Hynobius keyserlingi*, has extended its range into Europe.

Hynobius keyserlingi (Dybowski)   **Siberian Salamander**
1870 *Salamandrella keyserlingi* Dybowski
1910 *Hynobius keyserlingi* Boulenger
The wide range of this species traverses Siberia from west of

the Urals to the Kamchatka Peninsula and extends into adjacent Mongolia and Manchuria, as well as to Sakhalin Island and the Kuriles. In Europe, it has been recorded only from four localities in Russia. The first discovery was by Krassavzev (1931) near Gorsky (46° 13′ E, 58° 15′ N), the second by Turyeva (1948) near Siktivkar (approximately 51° E, 61° N), then again in 1965 by D. Nikiforov (Syroechkovskiy, 1966) near Yoshkar-Ola (approximately 48° E, 57° N), and finally by Nazarov (1968) on the River Polta, a tributary of the River Kuloy, a little way east of Archangel (43° 20′ E, 65° N). These localities are widely spread and it seems only a question of time before further populations are discovered.

Most of the range of this species is in the forest belt of northern Asia, typified by a mixture of conifers and birches. It is generally found in swampy areas in these forests in moss, under logs, or in rotting wood. In some areas, such as around Lake Baikal in east Siberia, it occurs in very large numbers. There are many records of specimens found asleep in permanently frozen ground in Siberia (Terentyev, personal communication, 1968).

The average length is about 4 to $4\frac{1}{2}$ in, and specimens up to $5\frac{1}{4}$ in have been recorded. The head is comparatively small and rather long in proportion to its width, with prominent 'cheeks' and a rounded snout. The eyes are large, prominent, and situated well forward. The neck is slender. The body is somewhat angular in section with twelve to fifteen (normally fourteen) distinct costal grooves. The tail, which is slightly shorter than the combined length of the head and trunk, is laterally compressed and bears a series of vertical grooves along each side. The limbs are moderately well-developed and all four feet have only four toes apiece. There is a distinct fold of skin across the rear of the throat. The skin over the whole surface is smooth and rather shiny.

On the dorsal surface the colour is uniform light brown, grading into a light grey on the underside. The sides and

limbs are marbled and speckled with black, these markings
tending to fuse dorsolaterally to form a distinct edge offsetting
the lighter dorsal colour.

Physical differences between the sexes are not always easy to
determine. The males have slightly longer limbs, and during
the breeding season develop low keels along the upper and
lower edges of the tail which sometimes persist at other times
of the year.

Very little is known about the habits of this salamander
except that it is very secretive when on land and normally becomes active only at night. Like other members of the genus,
when disturbed it can move surprisingly quickly for so short-
legged a creature, literally running with strong and almost
serpentine lateral undulations of the body. By the same
movements it can burrow into grass or moss very quickly.
Hibernation appears to take place on land.

Like most urodeles, the Siberian Salamander feeds largely
on soft-bodied prey such as small slugs, insect larvae, and
earthworms. The gape is not particularly wide and the size of
prey which can be swallowed is limited.

Reproductive maturity is reached during the third or sometimes the fourth year. In early spring, as soon as the ice has
disappeared, the salamanders repair to water, usually choosing
still, shallow pools. The female lays two spindle-shaped gelatinous sacs, each about 6 in long and $\frac{3}{4}$ in across and containing
about 50 or 60 eggs. A number of females often congregate in
one area to lay their eggs and the males fertilise them by dis-
charging sperm while swimming to and fro over the eggs.
According to Hellmich (1956) the egg-sacs are attached to
plants or twigs in such a manner that the top of each is just
above the surface of the water, in which the bottom end of the
sac dangles. It would seem, however, that this observation
might have resulted from a lowering of the water-level having
left the eggs slightly exposed, as more normally the eggs are
laid attached to twigs, plants, and stones completely sub-

merged. Initially, each egg inside the sac is further enclosed in a separate gelatinous envelope, but by the time the eggs are commencing to hatch (which takes about three or four weeks from the time of laying at average temperatures) the inner envelope has disappeared and the outer cover of the sac is also beginning to disintegrate. The tadpoles are therefore easily able to release themselves from the capsule and take up an active aquatic existence. At this stage they measure a little under ½ in in length and have well-developed external gills as well as prominent crests above and below on the laterally flattened tail, the upper crest continuing some way on to the back. The larvae are excellent swimmers and easily able to pursue the small water creatures on which they feed. Most larvae complete their growth to leave the water during late summer, but it is very probable that in the north of the range metamorphosis is frequently delayed over the winter.

CHAPTER 4

The Family Salamandridae

THIS is the most widespread of all the families of tailed amphibians, being represented in practically every part of the Northern hemisphere where urodeles are found at all. In Asia, Europe, and North Africa it is the dominant family, and it is well represented in North America. As can be seen from the list at the end of Chapter 2 (see p 39), of the nine genera and nineteen species of tailed amphibians found in Europe, six genera and sixteen species belong to this family. In fact, except in two comparatively small areas in Russia and South Europe respectively, any naturally occurring tailed amphibian found in this continent is bound to be a salamandrid. The European range of the family stretches from Ireland to the Urals and from the whole European coast of the Mediterranean almost to the Arctic Circle.

The salamandrids are generally small, the largest species growing to about 1 ft in length but many being only about 4 in long. Both the upper and the lower jaws contain teeth, and in addition the palate is furnished with two long rows of teeth which either lie parallel to each other or diverge posteriorly. The limbs and eyelids are well developed, and the tail may be either round in section or laterally compressed. The skin in some species is covered with small warts but in others is quite smooth. All species are furnished with skin glands which secrete an irritative or poisonous liquid of varying efficacy, in some species having little effect on most predators but in others obviously acting as a noticeable deterrent. Respiration is mainly carried out by means of well developed lungs in the adults, but is often supplemented by direct intake of oxygen through the skin or a vascular lining of the mouth and throat, particularly while the animal is in water. In a few cases, lungs are absent.

Fertilisation is internal. Generally, the adults are more or less terrestrial and resort to water in spring and early summer for breeding. Following an elaborate courtship display, distinctive for each species, the male emits a small gelatinous capsule known as a spermatophore, and this is picked up by the female with the cloaca and in most species stored until required for fertilisation of the eggs in a special receptacle

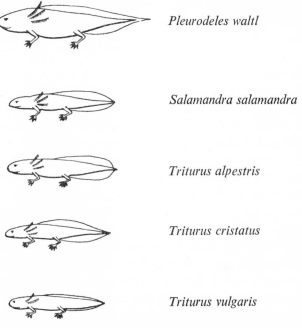

Pleurodeles waltl

Salamandra salamandra

Triturus alpestris

Triturus cristatus

Triturus vulgaris

Fig 2　Comparison of well-developed larvae
of five salamandrid species

known as the spermatheca. The eggs, usually laid singly and attached to plants, sticks, or stones, hatch out into gill-bearing tadpoles, which grow first the front and then the back legs and finally, following atrophy of the gills, emerge from the water as lung-breathing adults. In some cases the young are born alive, either as tadpoles or in the adult form. In several species a condition known as neotony has been observed, in which the larvae reach maturity without developing lungs, retaining the gills and remaining permanently aquatic.

GENUS *SALAMANDRA LAURENTI*

This genus is confined to Europe, West Asia and north-west Africa. It is represented in Europe by two species, *S. atra* in the Alps and western Balkans and *S. salamandra*, the latter's eight recognised subspecies covering all of South Europe and much of Central Europe. The genus is not represented in the British Isles or north of a line drawn roughly level with the southern-most edge of the Baltic.

The members of the genus are of moderately heavy build with a broad head and a sub-cylindrical tail. The sides of both body and tail bear a series of pronounced vertical grooves. The front legs have four toes; the third (counting from the inside) is the longest, the next longest is the second, then comes the fourth, and the shortest is the first. The hind legs have five toes; the third and fourth are the longest and more or less equal in length, while the first and fifth are the shortest. The toes bear little or no trace of webs, nor is there at any time a trace of the crests on the back and tail which are so prominent a feature of the genus *Triturus*, particularly in the males during the breeding season. Behind the eyes, in the temporal region, the head bears a pair of large and prominent paratoid glands, dotted with large pores. A double row of somewhat similar pores runs the length of the spine, and there is a further single row along each upper flank. The iris of the eye is dark. The tongue is circular and free on the sides. The vomero-palatine teeth are in two S-shaped rows diverging posteriorly and extending forward of the nostrils.

The habits of all the adult members of the genus are somewhat similar. They are nocturnal or crepuscular in habit, not normally active during the daytime except sometimes during and after rain. They require damp conditions for survival but are essentially terrestrial and do not normally enter water except that the females of *S. salamandra* at least repair to the edges of pools and ponds once a year to deposit their larvae in the water.

The young are born alive, but whereas in *S. atra* they enter the world as miniature replicas of their parents, the young of *S. salamandra* are born as gill-bearing tadpoles which after a period of aquatic existence metamorphose into the adult form and leave the water to continue their life on land.

Salamandra salamandra (Linnaeus)   **European Salamander**
1758 *Lacerta salamandra* Linnaeus
1768 *Salamandra maculosa* Laurenti
1827 *Salamandra vulgaris* Cloquet
1896 *Salamandra salamandra* Lönnberg

The range in Europe is as given for the genus. It is obvious that during at least the last glacial period the range of this species was broken up into small remnant areas and the population limited to a number of groups each contained in one or other of the refuges along the Mediterranean. This has resulted in considerable diversification of the species, so that it is now possible to recognise eight subspecies in Europe alone, of which six still remain more or less limited to the refuges while the other two have spread out widely into Central Europe. Other subspecies are found in West Asia and along the Mediterranean coast of north-west Africa.

The main requirements of this salamander are shade and moisture. Throughout most of its range, it has a predilection for wooded areas, particularly in hilly country. The nature of the soil and vegetation is of great importance, this species preferring deciduous woods with leaf litter, such as beech forests, and mostly avoiding coniferous forests on dry soils. It is often found at quite considerable elevations, up to 3,000 ft in some localities. However, it is usually most abundant in moderately elevated, hilly areas with suitable vegetation, and decreases in numbers at both greater and lesser elevations. In Germany, for example, it is quite common in such regions as the Harz foothills and the wooded hills near Minden, but slightly further north in the North German plain is generally found only in more or less isolated colonies in particularly suitable localities.

It is virtually impossible to confuse this salamander with any other, for its coloration is so striking. This will be obvious from the following general description, which is applicable to all the subspecies. The subspecific differences are given later when the European subspecies are dealt with separately.

The head is moderately depressed and nearly as broad as it is long. The snout is rounded and the nostrils equidistant from the tip of the snout and the eyes. The paratoid glands are particularly large and distinct and are furnished with many small pores. The trunk is stout and either round in section or slightly depressed in the middle. There is a pronounced gular fold across the throat. A somewhat irregular double row of large raised pores runs along the middle of the back and tail, one row on each side of the vertebral line, and a further series of such pores is dotted along the flanks and continues on to the cheeks. The limbs and toes are rather thickset, the latter being almost stubby. There are usually 22 to 25 vertebrae. The average length of adults is between $5\frac{1}{2}$ and $6\frac{1}{2}$ in, but much larger specimens, even exceeding 12 in, have been recorded, particularly in the southern part of the range. Normally, the tail is a little shorter than the combined length of the head and trunk, and the head is a little more than a quarter the length of

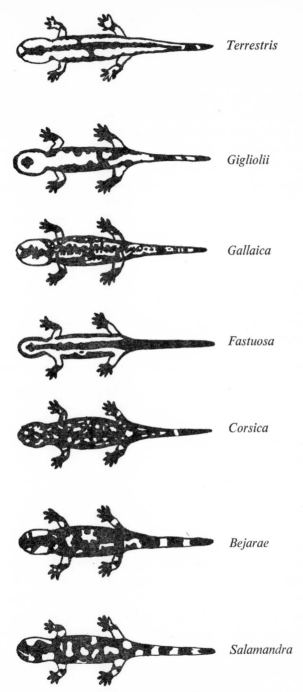

Fig 3   Typical patterns of subspecies of
Salamandra salamandra

the trunk alone. As an example, in a fairly large specimen measuring $7\frac{1}{2}$ in overall, the head was just under 1 in long, the trunk was just over 3 in, and the tail was $3\frac{1}{2}$ in long. The colour is shiny black, vividly marked in the upper surface with large yellow-to-orange blotches or stripes (Fig 3). The black of the under surface tends to be brownish or bluish, normally uniform but occasionally with small yellowish markings. There is always some yellow on the throat and on the upper surface of the limbs. There is no difference in coloration or pattern between the sexes, but the trunk of the male is normally shorter and more slender than that of the female, and the lips of the cloaca are more protuberant in the male.

Pairing has been observed to take place at almost all times of the year except when the salamanders are in hibernation, but usually occurs in spring or early summer and to a lesser extent in autumn. In captive specimens it has been seen to take place both on land and in the water, but in the wild state it probably nearly always occurs on land. The adults of this species are in any case by no means at home in the water. Pairing proper is often preceded by what virtually amounts to a period of chase, when the male actively pursues the female, butts her with his snout, and even sometimes bites her. The two sexes probably find each other at this time by smell, as a distinct odour from mating salamanders of this species has been reported by several observers, one of whom has likened it to the smell of liverwort (Dürigen, 1897). The male finally pushes himself under the female until she is lying on his back, and adopts a position of amplexus by raising his front legs and hooking them over those of the female. While in this position he emits a spermatophore which is taken up by the female with her cloaca. The method whereby this is achieved seems to vary. Some observers report that on occasion the male twists his body so that his cloaca is applied to that of the female, and the spermatophore is transferred direct from one to the other, but it would seem that often the male merely deposits the sperma-

Page 53   Danube Crested Newt *T. cristatus dobrogicus* (male)
                Danube Crested Newt *T. cristatus dobrogicus* (female)
                Marbled Newt *Triturus m. marmoratus* (male)
                Marbled Newt *Triturus m. marmoratus* (female)

Page 54   Palmate Newt *Triturus h. helveticus* (male)
              Palmate Newt *Triturus h. helveticus* (female)
              Carpathian Newt *Triturus montandoni* (male)
              Carpathian Newt *Triturus montandoni* (female)

tophore and it is subsequently found and taken up by the female.

Gestation requires several months and the young are mostly born in the spring. The female repairs to water for the purpose, choosing almost invariably either a cool, clear stream or a pond or pool which is fed by running water. She takes up a position, normally at the edge of the water, in which the tail and most or all of the body are immersed, but the head is clear of the water. The young are born alive, either enclosed in a transparent membrane from which they free themselves in the water, or already having broken out of the membrane shortly before birth. The number born at one time varies considerably, being usually between fifteen and twenty-five, often as many as fifty, and, rarely, as many as seventy-five. The young at birth are about 1 in long and in a comparatively advanced state of development, in that they are already furnished with four well-developed legs and shortly after birth are able to swim about quite actively. The external gills are quite prominent at birth and consist of three fairly long, feathery appendages on each side of the rear of the head, which as the larva develops tend to become more bushy and shorter in proportion to the animal's size. The tail is proportionately longer than in the adult (being approximately the same length as the head and trunk combined), is flattened laterally, and bears a wide crest along both its upper and lower edges, the upper crest extending forward along the body to about the middle of the trunk (see Fig 2). Both crests end fairly abruptly at the end of the tail, thus giving this organ a blunt, somewhat paddle-like appearance. Altogether, this forms an efficient swimming organ, and the larvae are indeed capable of quite rapid movements in the water. The colour of the larvae is brownish, darker above than beneath and often tinged with yellow on the flanks, while the whole is speckled with shiny black dots, which in some lights make the creature appear to be covered with minute sequins. As the larva grows, the body becomes stouter and the head

D

broader, the tail thickens in the centre and the crests diminish, and finally the gills atrophy, the lungs develop, and the young salamander leaves the water. A few days before final metamorphosis the colour commences to change quite noticeably, first becoming a darker brown and finally and quite rapidly the yellow markings appearing and the ground colour becoming almost or quite black. The first yellow patches to start appearing are those on the upper surface of each upper arm and thigh, and these markings are the most constant feature in the pattern of the adults of all subspecies.

The period of time from birth to metamorphosis is normally about three months but is subject to considerable variation, largely it would seem as a direct result of temperature. If the water is warm enough, the whole process may be completed in two months; on the other hand, young born too late to leave the water before the cold weather of winter will defer their metamorphosis until the following spring or early summer, and it is sometimes possible to find newly born young and the survivors from the previous year together in the same body of water, the latter being two or three times as long as the former. This may be one of the reasons why the size of freshly metamorphosed salamanders varies somewhat, the average being about $2\frac{1}{2}$ in long. Once having left the water, the young salamanders do not normally return to it again except temporarily for the females when breeding, and they become capable of this when about four years old.

The larvae commence feeding on quite small water-creatures such as *Cyclops* and *Daphnia*, which are actively pursued in the water or snapped up as they swim by. When a little larger the larvae take a wide range of small crustaceans, insect larvae, worms, and the like. Adult salamanders eat worms, slugs, grubs, and various insects, but generally prefer soft-bodied prey and avoid hard-shelled creatures such as beetles. The prey is seized by a sudden lunge and gulped down to the accompaniment of quite violent shakes of the head. A favourite is the small 'white slug', possibly because it is softer than many darker kinds of slug; the slime does not incommode the salamander, though following such a meal some time is spent in cleaning the jaws by wiping them on the ground or on vegetation.

It is usually considered that the striking coloration of this salamander serves as a warning of the poisonous effects of its skin secretions. Many experimenters have shown that the venom is of a composite nature, largely affecting the nervous system, though its main defensive value is presumably the irritative effect it can have on the skin, and more particularly on mucous membranes such as the lining of the mouth, of animals which attack the salamander. Most would-be predators undoubtedly find the salamander unpalatable for this reason, and many cases are on record of small animals such as lizards having died after having bitten one. Even such amphibian-eaters as the three European species of the snake genus *Natrix* rarely attack this salamander, though they have been known to eat it without apparent ill-effects. On the other hand, there is evidence to suggest that it can be fatal to other related snakes from outside its range.

SALAMANDRA SALAMANDRA SALAMANDRA (*LINNÉ*)
SPOTTED SALAMANDER

1768 *Salamandra maculosa* Laurenti
1897 *Salamandra maculosa nigriventris* Dürigen
1911 *Salamandra salamandra salamandra* Poche

This subspecies has the most extensive range of all the European subspecies of *S. salamandra*. It would appear to have spread into Central Europe from the Balkans or even possibly from Asia Minor, where its present southern boundary is in the region of Haifa in Israel. It has mainly extended north-west, enabling it to occupy the whole of the Balkans, part of West Russia, Hungary, Austria, and much of Germany, apart from the more westerly areas. Its western boundary runs through Switzerland and continues south to the Gulf of Genoa, in one or two places entering into France. The inland boundary of this subspecies still needs a certain amount of clarification, for two reasons. One is that particularly in the east of its range the boundary is in places not yet properly recorded, and the other is that over fairly large areas it intergrades with other subspecies. The more important of these areas of intergradation are in Central Germany and around the Gulf of Genoa, in both of which it intergrades with the subspecies *terrestris*, and at the eastern end of the Mediterranean, where it hybridises freely with *infraimmaculata*.

The yellow areas are considerably reduced in the coloration of this subspecies, compared with most of the others, and consist of a number of fairly large spots, irregular in shape, size and distribution, over the entire upper surface including the flanks. In some parts of the range the yellow tends to be orange, and even occasionally red. The effects of intergradation mentioned above appear to affect the pattern of the markings even well outside the areas of recognisable hybridisation, so that in the north-west part of the range, for example, the blotches tend to be more symmetrical than is normal elsewhere.

SALAMANDRA SALAMANDRA ALMANZORIS *MÜLLER & HELLMICH* 1935   CENTRAL SPANISH FIRE SALAMANDER

This is one of the several recognised subspecies limited to the Iberian Peninsula. It is found only in a small area in the Sierra de Gredos in Central Spain and is remarkable for the facts that it is found at a high altitude and has adopted a highly aquatic existence in various mountain lakes. In the Laguna de Gredos it lives at an altitude of over 6,500 ft, and it is also found in the Cincos Lagunas in the same area.

It is a comparatively small form and in conformity with its aquatic habits the tail is somewhat compressed laterally. Its main colour is a dingy black, the yellow markings being very much reduced. Hibernation takes place at the bottom of the lakes in which it lives, and during the warmer part of the year when it is more active it surfaces regularly for air. Little is known about its breeding habits.

SALAMANDRA SALAMANDRA BEJARAE *WOLTERSTORFF*

SPANISH FIRE SALAMANDER

1934 *Salamandra maculosa bejarae* Wolterstorff
1940 *Salamandra salamandra bejarae* Mertens & Müller

In Spain, to which country it is restricted, this is the commonest subspecies; it does not inhabit the northern strip comprising Galicia, the Cantabrian Mountains, and the Pyrenees, nor the extreme south of Spain, but is otherwise generally present.

It is a fairly large, robust form with a broad head, noticeably pointed snout and rather short tail, slightly compressed laterally. The yellow blotches are highly irregular and particularly those on the back tend to fuse to form V-shaped or U-shaped markings. Nearly always, there is a separate patch covering each paratoid gland and partly or entirely coloured red, in contrast to the yellow colour of the other markings.

Like all other subspecies except *almanzoris*, the adults are terrestrial in habit and frequent wooded areas for preference, so that in some parts of Central Spain where woods are infrequent the distribution is patchy.

SALAMANDRA SALAMANDRA CORSICA *SAVI*

CORSICAN FIRE SALAMANDER

1838 *Salamandra corsica* Savi
1839 *Salamandra moncherina* Bonaparte
1918 *Salamandra salamandra corsica* Nikolskiy

This form is limited to the island of Corsica, where it is the only representative of the species.

It is a strongly built, rather thick-bodied form, which tends to grow rather larger than most other subspecies, regularly reaching a length of 7 to 8 in and sometimes more. The head is very broad with a fairly blunt snout and small paratoids. As in *bejarae* the tail is rather short and slightly compressed laterally. The digits are somewhat stubby and flattened, and slightly webbed. The black ground colour is probably more predominant than in any of the other terrestrial subspecies, the yellow markings being comparatively small (except that those on the paratoids are often much larger), irregular in shape, and distributed with little or no evidence of any pattern.

As regards both build and pattern, this subspecies differs so much from any of those found on the adjacent European mainland that it hardly seems possible that it could have branched off from a common stock as late as the last inter-glacial, and it is tempting to think that it became isolated in its present home during an earlier glacial period. It is now generally accepted that the drop in sea level due to locking up of water in the polar ice-cap during the last glacial period was about 600 ft (Termier, 1958) and judging by present depths in the Mediterranean this would still have left a channel between Corsica and the Italian mainland roughly 10 miles wide at its narrowest point. Certainly this would have been an effective barrier for any urodele, and it may well be that the subspecies *corsica* has been isolated for a much longer period than at least some of the other subspecies. On the other hand, a fall in sea-level of only 300 ft could unite Corsica and Sardinia, and there is no obvious reason why the latter island should not be included in the range of the species.

SALAMANDRA SALAMANDRA FASTUOSA *SCHREIBER*

PYRENEAN FIRE SALAMANDER

1912 *Salamandra maculosa fastuosa* Schreiber
1940 *Salamandra salamandra bernadezi* Mertens & Müller
1940 *Salamandra salamandra bonnali* Mertens & Müller
1958 *Salamandra salamandra fastuosa* Eiselt

This subspecies occupies a strip of country along the north coast of Spain, taking in the Cantabrian Mountains as far west as the town of Lugo and extending eastwards through the West and Central Pyrenees roughly as far east as Andorra. It may therefore be considered a mountain form, but is mostly found in wooded areas at moderate elevation.

It is relatively small and slender with a proportionately long and slender tail. The head is short from front to rear, with a small rounded snout. The colour pattern is fairly regular, consisting normally of two yellow lines running one along each side of a central black line which extends from between the eyes along the back and on to the tail. The yellow lines are irregularly indented along their margins and may be as wide as the central black stripe, but are more often narrower. They may run on to the side of the tail but more normally stop short at the base of the tail, leaving the latter entirely black. The sides of the head and neck, as well as the snout and paratoids, are usually entirely yellow.

SALAMANDRA SALAMANDRA GALLAICA *SEOANE*

PORTUGUESE FIRE SALAMANDER

1884 *Salamandra maculosa gallaica* Seoane
1889 *Salamandra maculosa molleri* Bedriaga
1925 *Salamandra salamandra gallaica* Mertens

In Portugal, this is the common form of the species, and its range also extends northwards to include the extreme north-west corner of Spain. It intergrades with *bejarae* over a wide area extending along most of the eastern boundary of Portugal, and with *fastuosa* over a small area in the north-west of the peninsula. In build, it is rather similar to *bejarae*, with which it appears to be closely related, but tends to grow larger, the body being particularly stout. On the other hand, the tail is comparatively short, more or less equal in length to the distance between the angle of the mouth and the hind legs, with very little taper and quite blunt at the tip. In spite of its massive proportions, therefore, this subspecies rarely attains an unduly great overall length, and the average size of adult specimens no more than about 5 or 6 in. The head is quite distinct from the body, the top being flattened forward of the eyes but strongly developed posteriorly, with large paratoids. The snout is long and rather pointed. The fingers and toes are somewhat compressed and devoid of any trace of webbing.

The pattern makes this subspecies easy to identify, although it varies considerably in different individuals. The yellow markings on the back tend to form horseshoes or circles, and the areas enclosed by them are frequently dark grey or brownish or even reddish, in contrast to the black or bluish ground colour of the body. These markings may be irregularly distributed over the entire dorsal surface, but in many specimens have a tendency to fuse together to form an irregular longitudinal stripe along each side of the vertebral line. In effect, taking the normal pattern of *bejarae* as one extreme and that of *fastuosa* as the other, *gallaica* and its intergrades with the other two subspecies show in different individuals quite literally each stage in gradation between the two. Small markings on the flanks, limbs, tail, throat, eyelids, and paratoids may be yellow or red, and the whole throat is sometimes either bright red or tinged with red. The underside of the body frequently bears yellow dots, sometimes in great profusion.

SALAMANDRA SALAMANDRA GIGLIOLII *EISELT & LANZA 1956*
ITALIAN FIRE SALAMANDER

This form occupies the whole of the Italian Peninsula from the eastern Ligurian Apennines to the extreme south of Calabria. It was for a long time not distinguished from *S. s. salamandra* but is now usually regarded as sufficiently different to warrant separate subspecific status. The difference in pattern is most noticeable in the southern part of the range, and it may well be that this form was isolated in Italy during the last glacial period and evolved a distinctive form, but that following the spread of *salamandra* from the south-east refuge and the contact eventually established between the two forms in extreme northern Italy, a certain amount of 'gene-flow' has had the effect of ironing out the differences between the two over a larger area.

Gigliolii is rather smaller and more slender than *salamandra*. The head is broad and somewhat flattened, and the tail is rather long and narrow. In the northern part of the range, the colour pattern is fairly similar to that of *salamandra*, though with a tendency for the yellow markings to spread out and fuse to form very irregular blotches, often angular or extended. This tendency for the yellow markings to increase in size becomes progressively more noticeable towards the southern part of the range, and goes so far that in Calabria the upper surface is more or less entirely yellow, leaving only a certain amount of black on the flanks (which may send a few irregular extensions of black on to the dorsal surface) and often a central black patch on the head. Also in the southern part of the range, there is a general tendency for the yellow to be tinged with red, particularly on the lower flanks.

SALAMANDRA SALAMANDRA TERRESTRIS *LACÉPÈDE*

BANDED SALAMANDER

1788 *Salamandra terrestris* Lacépède
1883 *Salamandra maculosa europaea* Bedriaga
1897 *Salamandra maculosa taeniata* Dürigen
1897 *Salamandra maculosa quadrivirgata* Dürigen
1940 *Salamandra salamandra taeniata* Mertens & Müller
1958 *Salamandra salamandra terrestris* Eiselt

After *S. s. salamandra*, this subspecies has the widest range of all the eight European forms which are recognised to have subspecific status. In fact, *salamandra* and *terrestris* between them cover a greater area of Europe than all the other subspecies together. It is therefore of interest to note that they are the only races which have succeeded in occupying any of that part of Europe from which the species must have been driven during the last glaciation, and their spread has perhaps been facilitated by the absence of other forms in these areas. One notable feature, however, is that while *salamandra* still occupies the south-east refuge as part of its range, *terrestris* is the one subspecies whose present range is entirely, though in places only just, outside the three main refuge areas.

Superficially, *terrestris* probably resembles *fastuosa* more than any of the other forms, and has a common boundary with it along the northern edge of the Pyrenees. It is therefore possible that *terrestris* separated from *fastuosa* fairly recently and survived the last glaciation in north-east Spain, subsequently spreading into France and parts of Germany, but being pushed out of its foothold in Spain by other subspecies as the climate turned warmer. There is, however, another possibility which cannot altogether be discounted. This is that the home of *terrestris* during the last period of glaciation may have been North Italy, and that it subsequently spread northwards, but the later arrival of *salamandra* from the south-east forced it out of a wide area around the continental portion of Italy. The present range of *salamandra* certainly suggests that it has won ground from *terrestris* in Central Germany, and the large areas in which the two subspecies intergrade, particularly in Central and South Germany, would seem to indicate that considerable competition between them is still taking place. The varied colour pattern of *gigliolii* would give further slight support to this interpretation, as the prevailing pattern in the northern part of its range in Italy suggests a hint of *terrestris* as well as *salamandra* influence.

The present range of *terrestris* covers practically the whole of France, West Switzerland, parts of Belgium and Holland and much of West Germany. In the last country, it appears to be absent from the North Sea coastal strip as well as from the whole of Schleswig-Holstein except possibly a small area around Lauenburg and the extreme south of Holstein. East of this area, the boundary proceeds roughly south-east to skirt around the north and east of Berlin, then south more or less to the Czechoslovakian border, from there west through the Thuringian Forest, and south-west to the Rhone Valley. Much of this border between near Czechoslovakia and the Rhine is, however, difficult to determine accurately in view of the considerable confusion caused by the extensive intergradation in many places where the range of *terrestris* overlaps that of *salamandra*.

From the absence of the Banded Salamander in the British Isles, it may be assumed that it reached the area of the English Channel after the separation of England from the Continent, that is to say, not more than about 9,000 years ago (Zeuner, 1958). It is of course not impossible that it reached the British Isles before that date and died out subsequently, and reports of its having been found in England are not lacking (Fitter, 1959); but there is certainly no definite evidence to show that it has ever been a member of the British fauna.

Terrestris is a medium-sized race, on the average only slightly shorter than *salamandra* but decidedly more slender, though not to the same extent as *fastuosa* or *gigliolii*. The yellow markings on the back take the form of two parallel stripes, one on each side of a black vertebral stripe which is normally a little narrower than the yellow stripes. These yellow stripes may be either unbroken or broken at wide intervals, and run together part-way down the tail to form a single yellow stripe, almost invariably broken to a greater or lesser degree. Amendments to this pattern are sometimes found, often as local variants, including a tendency for the markings to be orange or red instead of yellow, the addition of two further yellow stripes on the lower flanks between the front and hind limbs, and an extension of the yellow on the dorsal surface to reduce or even replace the black. Rarely, completely black specimens have been found. The under surfaces of the head, throat, and body are often dark grey rather than black, sometimes with a variable number of dingy yellow spots; very occasionally, the ventral surface is entirely yellow or yellowish.

Salamandra atra (Laurenti) — Alpine Salamander

1768 *Salamandra atra* Laurenti
1850 *Salamandra nigra* Gray

As its common name indicates, this species inhabits the Alpine regions of Europe, in addition to which it is found in the mountainous areas on the western side of the Balkan Peninsula. The most westerly portion of its range lies near the Franco-Swiss border and takes in the northern half of the French Alps and parts of the French Jura. It is very abundant in many places in Switzerland, though strangely absent from a few apparently suitable localities, and ranges north as far as the Bavarian Alps and Würtemberg. Further east, the range includes parts of Austria and then follows a wide belt southeast across the north-east extremity of Italy and along the eastern side of the Adriatic into Albania.

The Alpine Salamander is rarely found anywhere below about 2,500 ft above sea-level and the absolute lowest level would appear to be about 1,900 ft. Above these heights, it is normally found at levels ranging up to about 6,000 ft and may in places reach almost 10,000 ft. Much of this range is well above the timber line, and while at lower levels the salamander may be found among tree roots and under logs in beech woods, in other places it spends most of its time under stones, in moss, and among low-growing vegetation. Although completely independent of water for breeding, its main essential requirement is moisture and it is never found in other than more or less damp places.

The average length of full-grown adults is around $4\frac{1}{2}$ in. Females are usually about an inch longer than males and occasionally reach a length of up to $6\frac{1}{2}$ in, but that seems to be about the limit. The general build is much more slender than that of *S. salamandra*. The head is rather flattened, nearly as broad as it is long, and with a rounded or slightly blunt snout. The paratoid glands are particularly well developed, about twice as long as they are broad and slightly enlarged posteriorly. The throat is not smooth as in *S. salamandra* but strongly wrinkled, often with a distinct fold across the rear margin. A series of distinct costal grooves along the slender body continues as a series of shallow grooves dividing almost the whole length of the tail into segments. A narrow double row of flattened glandular pores runs along the vertebral line from behind the head on to the base of the tail, and along each flank is a further single row of such pores forming much more pronounced protuberances than those on the back. The well developed limbs are smooth, though the joints of the rather flattened toes are often marked by distinct skin-folds. The tail is slender and slightly angular in section, often with a slight furrow running along the underside. The underside of the body proper is smooth.

The colour of the Alpine Salamander, which distinguishes it immediately from all other European urodeles, is a uniform glossy black above and below.

Apart from being on the average shorter than the female, the male is slightly more slender and can otherwise be distinguished by the rather more prominent cloacal lips.

Being adapted to cold, damp situations, this species is particularly sensitive to conditions which are too dry or too warm, and this may be in part responsible for the fact that it does not normally last very long in captivity at low levels. It is a very secretive creature which usually leaves its hiding-place only at night, but on occasions a spell of rain or heavy dew can result in surprisingly large numbers appearing on the surface in the daytime.

Like most other European newts and salamanders, it sloughs its old skin entire from time to time, and, having first freed its head and worked the skin down to the rear part of the body, seizes it in its jaws and swallows it.

The natural food of this salamander consists of soft-bodied creatures such as earthworms, slugs, and arthropods. The process of catching and swallowing the prey is similar to that described for *S. salamandra* (see p 56).

Although closely related to *S. salamandra*, which it replaces in its range at about 2,500 ft, the Alpine Salamander has acquired an even greater independence from water in that the young are born alive on land in the adult form and have no need to pass through any aquatic larval stage. The adults require two to three years to achieve full size (growth taking somewhat longer at higher than at lower levels) and become capable of reproduction at three or four years of age. Pairing takes place as a rule in July or August and involves a form of amplexus in which the male lies lengthwise along the back of the female and hooks his front legs over hers. During amplexus, the female mostly remains passive but may occasionally move about, literally carrying the male on her back. The period of gestation is quite a long one, lasting about a year at lower levels, and, at higher levels, at which the period of hibernation becomes increasingly longer, taking two or even three years. Although only two (or rarely three or four) young are born at a time, the ovaries are comparatively large and do in fact each produce at each gestation anything between ten and twenty-five eggs, which descend into the respective oviduct on each side. Of these, only one or rarely two eggs from each ovary develop (always those lying furthest from the ovary in the oviduct) and the remaining eggs lying behind them slowly break down into a fluid mass which eventually surrounds the developing egg and is absorbed by it to provide nourishment for the embryo.

The developing larva goes through all the obvious stages of development which take place in the aquatic larvae of other tailed amphibians, including the development of bright red external gills and a laterally compressed tail. The gills in fact seem to have been adapted for quite a different use and develop in the unborn larva to a far greater size than in any of the normally aquatic larvae of other species, reaching at their maximum development approximately half the total length of the larva. At this stage, they are pressed against the wall of the uterus and it would seem that they function as a primitive placenta to obtain food and oxygen from the bloodstream of the mother. The young are usually born within a few hours of each other, but the births may on occasion be separated by a period of several days, which presumably is due to a 'take-over' which it would seem can occur in the early stages of gestation. If for any reason the initial egg in the oviduct fails to develop, the next egg in the row can develop in its place instead of degenerating as it would otherwise have done. This would seem to indicate that all the eggs, both those which develop and those which do not, are normally fertilised, but it is of course not possible for this replacement of the developing egg to take place once the remaining eggs have commenced to degenerate. Presumably some slight maladjustment of this mechanism is the cause of the rare cases in which two embryos from one ovary develop to full term.

At birth, the young are about 2 in long and in every other way resemble the parents, the gills by this time having been absorbed and the tail having assumed a more cylindrical form.

GENUS *CHIOGLOSSA BOCAGE*

This is a monotypic genus, separated as such largely on account of skeletal differences and its rather specialised tongue (Noble, 1931).

Chioglossa lusitanica Bocage 1864

Gold-striped Salamander

The range of this species is limited to the more northerly portion of Portugal and adjacent areas in north-west Spain from Galicia to Old Castile.

Within its limited range, the species is even more restricted by its rather specialised habitat preferences, which in some areas cause it to be found only in isolated colonies. It appears to be properly at home only at fairly high elevation and is rarely found at low levels. A typical habitat is a well-wooded rocky area, usually on the side of a valley, where springs and small streams are plentiful. Abundant moisture and high air humidity seem to be necessary, and no doubt these exacting requirements have been largely instrumental in keeping the species confined to what was presumably its refuge during the last glaciation, since the proximity of the Atlantic to this rather mountainous area makes it one of the wettest parts of the Iberian Peninsula.

This is a fairly small salamander, its total length averaging between 4 and 5 in, with a maximum of about 6 in. The body is so slender that it appears elongated and the tail is likewise thin and quite long, from one and a half to twice as long as the snout-vent length, and sharply pointed at the end. Both body and tail are almost cylindrical, except that the posterior part of the tail is slightly compressed laterally. The vomero-palatine teeth are in two longitudinal rows, double-curved in a flattened 'S' shape. The sides of the body bear a series of vertical grooves, usually ten to eleven on each side, which are continued as shallower and smaller but still quite distinct grooves on the sides of the tail. The skin is smooth with no tuberculosities or skin appendages; there is, however, a fold of skin across the throat. The base of the tail in the male is noticeably swollen.

The brownish or blackish ground colour of the back and sides is strikingly relieved by two longitudinal orange or copper-coloured stripes, of almost metallic appearance, which join together behind the hind legs to continue as a single stripe to the end of the tail. The undersides are uniform light brown or grey.

The tongue is very specialised, being quite large in propor-

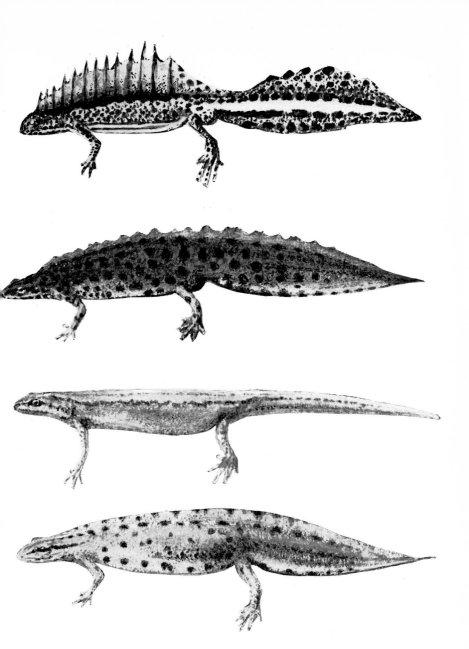

Page 71   Banded Newt *Triturus vittatus* (male)
            Smooth Newt *Triturus v. vulgaris* (male)
            Smooth Newt *Triturus v. vulgaris* (female)
            Southern Smooth Newt *T. vulgaris meridionalis* (male)

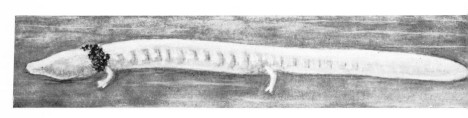

Page 72　Spectacled Salamander *Salamandrina terdigitata*
Olm *Proteus anguinus*

tion to the animal's size, free behind and on the sides, and capable of considerable extension. Not only is *Chioglossa* quite lizard-like in general appearance, but it also has some lizard-like habits. It is more active than most urodeles and can run quite quickly. It stalks its prey rather in the manner of a chameleon (Hellmich, 1956). Being frequently found near water, it does not hesitate to escape into this medium if disturbed (Noble, 1931). It may occasionally be found wandering abroad in daylight, but normally emerges at dusk in search of its prey and spends the daytime hidden under moss or stones. It climbs about well among rocks and logs. Like many lizards and comparatively few amphibians, it is able to throw off its tail quite readily if this member is seized, and grow a new one in due course.

In the main, the food of this salamander consists of small insects such as flies. These it stalks and catches by shooting out the long sticky tongue. Small worms and grubs are also taken, but large worms and hard-shelled beetles are usually avoided. Small moths and spiders are taken readily, provided they are moving about slowly enough, since in spite of its surprising turn of speed, *Chioglossa* cannot overtake really fast-moving prey. There seems little doubt that it recognises the prey by its movement, as dead food is ignored, as is stationary prey unless it has already moved sufficiently to attract the salamander's attention.

Very little is known about the breeding habits of this species. It may be assumed that, as with other members of the family, fertilisation is internal and probably takes place on land following a period of courtship display and amplexus, similar to that described elsewhere (see p 52) for *Salamandra* (Noble, 1931). The eggs are laid in water, usually springs or streams with a moderate current being chosen. The larvae are active swimmers with a well developed tail.

E

GENUS *EUPROCTUS GENÉ* 1838

This genus is confined to Europe and consists of three species, living respectively in Corsica, Sardinia, and the Pyrenees. This area obviously suggests that the main stock from which these species derived was originally more widely spread in South Europe at least, was compressed and split up during one or other of the periods of glaciation, and has since been unable, as a result of its adaptation to a specialised habitat, to break out of its refuge areas, particularly since two of these have subsequently been isolated by sea.

All three species are adapted to life at high altitude in mountainous areas. They are able to withstand very low temperatures, and the fact that they rarely live long in captivity may well be due to an inability to tolerate high temperatures or low altitudes, or possibly both. The lungs are considerably reduced and oxygen intake must depend to a considerable extent on cutaneous respiration, which obviously suffices for the maintenance of life in a comparatively sluggish amphibian at low temperatures, but probably could not cope with the increased demand at higher temperatures.

These adaptations no doubt also fit in with the exigencies of an aquatic existence, but it is in fact not easy to say just how aquatic these animals are in their natural habitat. Most places where they are found are free from ice and snow only for four o. five months in the year, which roughly corresponds with the n rmal breeding season when most adults are in any case in the w ter, although not infrequently specimens are found on land, usually under stones and often quite a long way from water. During the rest of the year, conditions are such that observation of their habits is largely impossible, and whether most of them remain in the water under the ice or on land under the snow is by no means clear.

These are rather drab-coloured, small to medium-sized

salamanders, with a distinctive flat, broad head. The tail is strongly developed, particularly in the male, who is otherwise not noticeably different in build from the female.

Breeding takes place in the water, usually among rocks at the edge of streams and lakes. The male approaches the female and pushes his body under hers, at the same time twisting his tail around her body in the region of the hind-limbs or lower abdomen. The grip of the male's tail (Fig 4) is such that the

Fig 4   Tail-hold during courtship
in *Euproctus asper*

female is quite unable to free herself, and this position is maintained for rarely less than an hour and has been known to last (in captive specimens) as long as 28 hours (Ahrenfeldt, 1960). Normally, this period of amplexus concludes with the passing of a spermatophore from the cloaca of the male direct to that of the female. The eggs are laid in due course, after being internally fertilised in this manner. They are comparatively large and are attached singly by the female to the underside of stones, usually in running water though frequently among rocks at the edge of mountain lakes. The larvae, in common with those of most other mountain-brook salamanders, are streamlined in appearance, with short gills, and narrow tail-fins.

Although the larvae are capable of considerable activity at times, this can hardly be said of the adults, which are in general slow-moving and sluggish, whether in water or on land. This is reflected in their choice of food, since they appear to be incapable of catching anything other than slow-moving prey like earthworms and slugs, and, in the water, such grubs and other larvae as are found under the stones where the salamanders also spend much of their time.

Euproctus asper (Dugès)   Pyrenean Mountain Salamander
1852 *Hemitriton asper* Dugès
1885 *Euproctus asper* Camerano

This species is confined entirely to the Pyrenees, particularly to the central and eastern sections, very rarely in the western section. It is, however, not entirely restricted to Spain, as apart from being found also in Andorra, it extends its range just over the border into extreme south-west France. As with all species of *Euproctus*, it is confined to high altitudes, being rarely if ever found below about 2,000 ft and extending up to possibly 10,000 ft. In fact, within this overall range of altitude, it seems to prefer the higher levels, which subjects it generally to more rigorous climatic conditions than those endured by the other two species. In some localities, it is doubtful whether normal weather conditions allow the salamander to be active for more than four months in the year.

This species can easily be distinguished from the others in the genus by two characteristics—the quite rough and granulated nature of the skin, and the presence of a fold of skin across the throat. The average length of adults is 4 to 5 in, although specimens of over 6 in have been found. It is the largest and most robust in build of the three species. The hind-legs are strongly built and the tail is fairly thick throughout most of its length, tapering appreciably only towards its end. The ground colour is grey to black, sometimes with a greenish tinge, usually with a yellowish stripe along the centre of the back, and occasionally with a few scattered yellow spots. The undersides are orange-red in the female, and in the male yellowish except the cloacal region, which is dull grey. The upper and lower colours are separated by a series of dark spots. A narrow red or yellow stripe runs along the top edge of the tail. The lungs are quite small, and presumably would be inadequate except at low temperatures and in the oxygen-rich waters typical of the species' habitat (Noble, 1931).

Pairing takes place in June. The larvae have large yellowish-green spots on the back and sides, and a bright red lower edge to the tail-fin.

EUPROCTUS ASPER ASPER (*DUGÈS*)

1852 *Hemitriton asper* Dugès

1928 *Euproctus asper asper* Mertens & Müller

In 1925, Wolterstorff decided to recognise three local forms of the species as separate subspecies. At present, only one of these forms is still accorded subspecific status, and it is open to argument whether even this form deserves to be so recognised. However, accepting for the present that the separation into subspecies is justified, the main population of the species throughout most of the range is given trinomial status as *Euproctus a. asper*.

EUPROCTUS ASPER CASTELMOULIENSIS *WOLTERSTORFF 1925*

This, the only new form described by Wolterstorff to be still generally regarded as a separate subspecies, is confined to the Torrent de Castelmouly, near Bagneres de Bigorre, in the French Pyrenees. It differs only in the colour pattern, having normally a series of yellow spots on the back and sides. According to Thorn, who examined the subspecies in its native locality, the increase in yellow coloration is noticeable in juveniles, but adults vary little, if at all, from those from other areas (Thorn, 1961, private communication).

Euproctus montanus (Savi)   Corsican Mountain Salamander
1838 *Megapterna montana* Savi
1878 *Euproctus montanus* Gigliolii

Confined to Corsica, this salamander is found in or near mountain streams at elevations of approximately 2,000 to 8,000 ft. Occasional specimens found at lower levels may result from tadpoles carried downstream (Hellmich, 1956) but it does not seem that the species can breed at lower elevations than those at which it is normally found.

It is smaller than *E. asper*, its total length averaging about $3\frac{1}{2}$ to 4 in. The skin is comparatively smooth, lacking all or most of the warts and rugosities characterising *E. asper*, and also that species' gular fold. The head is also quite distinctive, the snout being blunt, and the rear of the head having a swollen appearance due both to the presence of noticeable paratoid glands and of a thickening of the skull bones in this region. The posterior third only of the tail is laterally compressed. The upper surfaces are olive-grey or brown, finely spotted or stippled in black or dark brown. A yellow or light brown dorsal stripe is usually present. The under surface is grey or brown, often covered with dark spots, except for the throat, which is normally uniform in colour.

Amplexus is similar to that in *E. asper*, and is presumably assisted by the development in the breeding season of a small spur on the fibula of the hind-leg in the males.

Euproctus platycephalus (Gravenhorst)
                    Sardinian Mountain Salamander
1829 *Molge platycephala* Gravenhorst
1838 *Euproctus rusconii* Gené
1839 *Euproctus platycephalus* Bonaparte

This species occurs in Sardinia in similar habitats to those occupied in Corsica by *E. montanus*, being found almost exclusively at high elevations in mountainous areas. It is most abundant in the Monte Gennargentu area, where it is found at heights of up to about 6,000 ft.

The average length of adults is about $4\frac{1}{2}$ in. The head appears noticeably flattened with a depressed and elongated snout whose shape is reflected in the common German name for the species—Hechtkopf-Gebirgsmolch or Pike-Headed Mountain Newt. The paratoid glands are so small as to be virtually unnoticeable. Body and limbs are slender and the tail, which constitutes at least half the total length, is strongly compressed laterally. The skin is granular. There is no gular fold. In the males, a spur-like process on the lower part of the hind-limb superficially resembles a sixth toe. The upper surface of the body is light to dark brown with chestnut blotches or spots, and usually has a pale yellowish or brownish vertebral stripe. Belly and throat are whitish or yellowish (usually more yellowish along the central line) and spotted with black, these spots tending to be more numerous and distinct in the males than in the females, where they are sometimes hardly noticeable.

The mating habits of this salamander are similar to those of the other two members of the genus except that the male, in addition to holding the female with his prehensile tail and hind-legs, seizes and holds her in his jaws, either just in front of or just behind the hind-legs. Breeding is said to take place twice a year, in late spring and early autumn.

GENUS *PLEURODELES MICHAHELLES* 1830

This genus is found only in North Africa and the Iberian Peninsula, and only one species is found in the European part of the range.

The members of the genus are comparatively large, robust salamanders, with large, broad heads, a rough skin, and a tendency for the tips of the ribs to protrude through the skin of the flanks. In habit, they are more aquatic than is the case with most genera in the family, and less active than many. Breeding is fairly typical of the family, involving a period of amplexus during which a spermatophore is passed from the male to the female, so that the eggs are laid already fertilised; the young pass through a normal tadpole stage, of generally longer duration than in other genera, before metamorphosing into the adult form.

Pleurodeles waltl Michahelles 1830   Iberian Ribbed Newt
This species is fairly widespread throughout the southern and western parts of the Iberian Peninsula, and is also found in some areas of Morocco.

It frequents ponds, lakes, swamps, and ditches, though not normally running water. In general, it prefers water with plentiful vegetation, where its slow-moving, bottom-dwelling habits make it difficult to detect. Although it is capable of moving around quite freely on land, it rarely leaves the water, and should the pool or pond in which it lives dry up temporarily, as frequently happens in Southern Spain, the salamander usually buries itself in the mud and stays there until the next rains.

This is without doubt the largest of the European tailed amphibians, fully-grown adults having an average length of 8 in and frequently reaching 12 in, while even 15 to 16 in is not unknown. The head has a somewhat square appearance, being roughly as broad as it is long (in females usually even broader but in males sometimes slightly less broad), with a bluntly rounded snout. Through being considerably flattened, having a distinctively swollen appearance behind the eyes, and being set straight on to the body without any neck, the head has some resemblance to that of a toad. In proportion to the size of the head, however, the eyes are comparatively small. The body is stout and rounded but the tail is strongly compressed laterally and makes up at least half the total length. Above and below, the tail is furnished with a narrow keel, and its end comes to a blunt point. The limbs are 'stocky'—strongly built but somewhat short. A prominent fold of skin is present across the throat. The skin is covered with numerous minute pores and has a rough, granular appearance, while a most noticeable feature is a row of large wart-like protuberances along each upper flank, each protuberance coinciding with the end of one of the ribs. These ribs are sharply pointed and it can sometimes happen that under slight pressure the needle-like points slightly protrude from the large warts, presumably acting as a protection against predators.

In colour, this salamander is dirty yellow to olive-green in young adults, and often a dark brownish grey in older specimens. The large warts on the flanks are usually picked out in dull orange, and the lower edge of the tail is often tinged with the same hue. The ground colour of the abdomen and throat is dirty white, sometimes with a yellowish tinge. The whole of the body is covered with more or less distinct irregular dark spots or blotches, which stand out more prominently against the lighter colour of the underside, though occasional specimens are found in which these spots are lacking. The males tend to have a fairly easily distinguishable reddish tinge on the body, noticeably longer tails than the females, and dark rugose pads on the underside of the upper arms. The body of the male is also rather more slender than that of the female, and the cloacal region is more swollen.

Voracious and by no means choosy, this large salamander feeds on almost anything that moves, from small insects to the largest of worms, and cannot be relied on to respect the larvae of other amphibians or even its own. On occasion, it has been known to attack adults of the smaller Bosca's Newt, which shares roughly the same range in the Iberian Peninsula.

The breeding season of this species is, to say the least, an extended one, as under suitable conditions it appears able to breed at almost any time of the year. Quite a wide variation of water temperature is tolerated; over most of its range really cold weather rarely occurs, so that the greatest factor inhibiting reproduction is probably drought. During courtship, the male swims or crawls under the female and lifts his front limbs to hook them over hers. This position may be maintained for several hours but eventually, by twisting the rear of his body forwards (often freeing one fore-leg for the purpose), the male deposits a spermatophore near the snout of the female. He then crawls forward, carrying the female with him, until the latter's cloaca is directly over the spermatophore, which she is thus able to pick up. The fertilised eggs, which are quite small for so large a salamander, are laid singly or more usually in small clumps, being attached by the female to plants or stones. Usually, some 200 to 300 eggs are laid at a time, and the female may lay eggs as many as four or five times during the year. The larvae reach a length of up to 4 in and metamorphose after about four months, though this period varies according to water temperature and other factors. Average adult size takes two to three years to attain.

GENUS *SALAMANDRINA FITZINGER* 1826

Only one species is included in this genus, so no separate description of it need be given.

Salamandrina terdigitata (Lacépède)   Spectacled Salamander
1788 *Salamandra terdigitata* Lacépède
1803 *Salamandra tridactyla* Daudin
1821 *Salamandra perspicillata* Savi
1826 *Salamandrina perspicillata* Fitzinger
1918 *Salamandrina terdigitata* Dunn
Apart from being confined to Europe, the range of the Spectacled Salamander is certainly a limited one. It occurs only in Italy, from Liguria in the north to the area of Naples in the

south, being most abundant around Genoa. Even in this limited range, it is confined to the mountain slopes along the west side of the Apennines. It prefers wooded areas, where it lives in the damp leaf litter under the trees, and normally remains near small streams.

It is a small salamander, measuring only about 3 in long. The head is set on a narrow neck and is slightly longer than it is wide, with a bluntly rounded snout. The eyes are prominent and quite large. It has a slender body, slightly squarish in section. The tail is long (more than half the total length), almost round, except for a slight lateral compression, pointed at the end, and furnished above and below with a low but sharp-edged ridge. The limbs are long and slender and each is furnished with only four toes. The long tongue, attached only at the front, can be extended well out of the mouth. The skin has a matt, rough appearance. Full-grown males are shorter than the females, with a shorter body and longer tail in proportion to the total length.

Above, the ground colour is dull black, relieved on top of the head by a yellowish or vermilion 'spectacle' mark shaped like a horseshoe with the open part forward and with the broad ends over the eyes. Beneath, the abdomen is dirty white with a few dark blotches, but the underside of the chin is white, the throat is black with a small white patch, and the anal region, the inner sides of the legs, and the lower edge of the tail are all bright red.

Except occasionally after rain the Spectacled Salamander rarely appears in daylight, but wanders abroad at dusk and after dark. Adults are essentially terrestrial except during the breeding season.

Little is known about the breeding habits of this species, but it is believed that mating takes place on land by means of a spermatophore deposited by the male and picked up by the female. The eggs are laid in early spring in small streams where the current is not too fast, and deposited in small clusters attached to stones. The form of the larvae is typical of the genus, except that the limbs develop with only four toes.

The normal food of adults consists of small insects, which are captured in rather toad-like fashion by means of the extensible sticky tongue. Larger insects, worms, and grubs are usually ignored, and a large part of the food of this species in the wild probably consists of quite small prey such as greenfly.

This is one of the many species of salamander in which the lungs are greatly reduced—to rudimentary organs about 2 mm long (Noble, 1931). This, as is often the case, may be regarded as an adaptation to environment, since large lungs reduce specific gravity and become a disadvantage in running water. Lung capacity is, moreover, not so necessary in a cool environment where a low rate of metabolism reduces oxygen need, particularly in mountain streams which are normally rich in oxygen, and cutaneous or buccopharyngeal respiration can more or less cope with requirements.

This appears to be another obvious case of a European amphibian bottled up in one of the southern refuges during the ice ages and becoming so adapted to life at low temperatures that it is unable to break out of its mountain habitat.

GENUS *TRITURUS RAFINESQUE* 1815

A few decades ago it could be said that this was the most widespread of all the urodele genera, with species in large areas of Europe, Asia, and North America. Since then, reasons have been found from time to time for splitting off various species and groups of species and creating new genera for them, so that the genus as it now stands is largely confined to Europe and overlaps only slightly into south-west Asia and northwest Africa. Nevertheless, inside Europe there can be no doubt that it is the dominant genus. The eight species and twenty-seven subspecies to be described cover most of the Continent, including the British Isles where no other genus is represented, and excluding only the northern fringe where climatic conditions are too severe. As it is, the genus ranges surprisingly far northwards, up to 63° N in places, as well as extending eastwards beyond the Urals. In several cases, it is easy to deduce how an original stock must have been split up during the glacial periods and subsequently formed separate subspecies or even species, some of which have since spread out again to overlap each other.

Although this genus belongs to the same family as most other European tailed amphibians, its members have a number of distinctive characteristics, and are commonly known as 'newts' rather than salamanders.

These newts depend on water for breeding; and, although many of them travel considerable distances between breeding seasons and during the two or three years which normally elapse between metamorphosis and sexual maturity, they are usually found near ponds and pools. They desiccate fairly readily and when out of water are limited to areas where the ground remains reasonably moist. The optimum habitat for large populations is a fair-sized pond, preferably with a slight flow of water, adjacent to deciduous woodlands. They are, however, by no means over-specialised, and a colony can often be found far from woods of any sort, or breeding in most unlikely bodies of water such as small ornamental ponds, shallow wells, or even sluggish streams. It is, however, necessary for both water of some sort and a satisfactory 'hinterland' to be available. Of the two, the latter is probably the more important in deciding the size of the colony, since if the requirements for the rest of the year are catered for, quite a small body of water can at times suffice for the breeding facilities of a comparatively large population. In general, large and deep ponds or lakes are unfavourable, probably in many cases because of the greater danger from predators such as large fish and because the need to surface for air limits the depth at which the newts can survive. Undoubtedly temperature is also a factor, as shallow water warms up in spring more quickly than deep water and too low a temperature retards both the onset of breeding and the development of the eggs and young.

The process of surfacing for air is similar for all species, and involves a quick swim to the surface and a rapid gulp of fresh air. Bottom-dwellers such as *T. cristatus* then tend to return at once to the bottom, while more free-swimming species such as *T. vulgaris* may often remain at or near the surface.

Most of the special characteristics of the genus are related more or less directly to reproduction. The adults of all the species spend the greater part of the year on land, though some tend to enter the water on occasion. Hibernation usually takes place on land and only occasionally in water. In all species, the adults take to the water around early spring for a period of a few months during which breeding occurs. At this time, noticeable changes in appearance take place, particularly in the males. The texture of the skin, which is dry and often velvety or matt in newts living on the land, changes to become more absorbent to water and acquires a more glossy appearance. In many species the colours become more vivid, and the comparatively drab hues of the terrestrial period change into patterns. Probably the most striking change is in the development in the breeding male of growths of skin, the most prominent in many species being a dorsal cutaneous crest extending from the rear of the head more or less to the end of the tail.

Fertilisation is internal but does not involve any form of amplexus. It is preceded by a characteristic courtship display by the male, slightly varying for each species. During this display, the male takes up a position in front of or to one side of the head of the female, presents one side towards her, folds the tail round towards that side and vibrates the end of the tail vigorously. It is now generally accepted that a major function of this tail-lashing is to impel a stream of water carrying odours released from certain male glands towards the female.

If she reacts suitably, which mostly involves passively remaining in position instead of moving away, the male ultimately deposits a spermatophore consisting of a mass of sperm-cells surrounded by a gelatinous covering. The female moves over the spermatophore and picks it up with her cloaca. Here the sperm-cells are released from the envelope and move up into a special receptacle where they are stored until the eggs are ready for fertilisation.

The eggs are laid singly, and as a rule the female takes considerable care in selecting a suitable place to deposit each egg. This is frequently the leaf of a water-plant or a blade of grass, and as the egg is laid the female uses her hind-legs and feet to fold the leaf around the egg, in which position it is fastened by its sticky covering. Eggs may also be deposited on bottom detritus, such as dead leaves or sticks, especially when the pool or pond contains no vegetation.

The eggs hatch out into small slender larvae which are capable of bursts of active swimming almost from birth. In due course the fore-legs appear, and subsequently the hind-legs. The form of the larvae in all species is generally similar, noticeable features being the three pairs of bushy external gills, and the cutaneous crests above and below the tail—the upper one extending on to the back, so that the depth of the tail is for most of its length at least equal to and mostly greater than the depth of the body. Metamorphosis takes place when the larvae are a few months old, or is otherwise delayed over winter until the following spring. A further two or three years are required before maturity is reached, and during this period the young newts remain essentially terrestrial.

These newts are of small to medium size (up to 6 or 7 in for the largest species), moderately slender, and with a tail more or less the same length as the body. The tongue is oval in shape and attached to the bottom of the mouth only along the median line. The vomero-palatine teeth are in two rows, almost parallel to each other but converging slightly anteriorly.

The tail is strongly compressed laterally, more particularly during the breeding season, when it constitutes an efficient swimming organ. There are four toes on each front limb and five on each hind limb. The skin is quite smooth in some species, rough in others, but there is no noticeable trace of paratoid glands or large glands on the body as are apparent in some of the other European salamanders.

The males may be distinguished from the females, apart from the differences in colour and skin appendages to be described for each species, by the formation of the cloaca, which in the male is dome-shaped (and considerably enlarged during the breeding season), and in the female flattened as though truncated.

Lateral line organs are present not only in the larvae but also in the adults, although they disappear under the skin during terrestrial periods and are then presumably functionless. The term 'lateral line organs' was first used in connection with fishes, many of which have a row of these sense organs along each side, and is here used for want of a better term. It is, however, rather a misnomer as far as the newts are concerned, since these organs are dotted irregularly on the back rather than on the sides, and are particularly abundant on the upper surface of the head.

The behaviour of these newts on land is very similar for all species. They are active at night, wandering around in search of food, and spend the daytime in damp places under stones, logs, moss, and leaf litter. In fact, certain aspects of their life on land, such as their migratory habits, have been very little studied, largely because they live a more secretive and less active life at this time than they do when in the water, and are correspondingly less easy to observe. The annual aquatic period for breeding usually lasts about three months, or for some species a little longer. At this time not only are the newts more active but there is a tendency for the activity to vary with different species, as will be further explained when each species

Page 89   (*above*) Head of Siberian Salamander *Hynobius keyserlingi*
(*below*) Eggs of Siberian Salamander *Hynobius keyserlingi*

Page 90   (*above*) Spanish Fire Salamander *Salamandra salamandra bejarae*. Female   (*below*) Head of Spanish Fire Salamander *Salamandra salamandra bejarae*

is described. These differences in behaviour are most notice-able when more than one species occupies the same body of water, as frequently happens. In many places in Germany, for example, *T. vulgaris, cristatus, helveticus*, and *alpestris* may be found breeding in the same pond, and even in England in cer-tain areas all three of the resident species occupy the same piece of water. As populations of several acres of land may crowd together into one small pond during the breeding season, and a particularly suitable pond may contain hundreds or even thousands of newts at this time, it seems probable that the different species, which behave similarly on land, behave differently from each other in the water—and this may allow each species to develop a larger population than it otherwise would. The differences in behaviour are noticeable: some species prefer deeper water than others, some are bottom-feed-ers and others feed to a considerable extent at or near the surface of the water, some depend rather more on their sense of smell to detect food while others rely mainly on eyesight, and so on.

All species slough the skin entire at regular intervals. The old skin first separates around the lips and is then rolled back along the body and tail, the limbs being withdrawn as they are reached. Sloughing is often assisted by rubbing against stones or crawling through thick vegetation, and it is quite common for the newt to seize the skin in its mouth when it is rolled back sufficiently far for this to be possible, and to swallow it when it is entirely removed. This is by no means difficult, as the cast skin is extremely thin and nearly transparent.

The food of all species consists almost entirely of small crea-tures such as insects, worms, and slugs. The larger newts tend to take comparatively large prey, which is seized in the jaws and swallowed by a series of gulps, usually accompanied by violent jerks of the body and shaking of the head from side to side. The smaller newts adopt the same technique when dealing with worms and larger insects, but on land also take small in-sects such as greenfly by protruding the tongue, to which the

F

insect adheres and is carried back into the newt's mouth. In most cases, only live prey is taken, but some smaller species, particularly *T. vulgaris*, have a habit of swimming near the surface and examining small floating objects, which will be seized if acceptable. In this way they account for large numbers of dead flies and similar small creatures which have fallen into the water and died. Instances have also been reported of newts eating frog's eggs and those of their own and other species of newt. The sense of smell is well developed in all the newts but more so in some than others, *T. cristatus* and *T. alpestris* being good examples of this. Most newts kept in captivity quickly detect small pieces of meat dropped into the water, and hunt around until they find them.

Triturus alpestris (Laurenti)   **Alpine Newt**
1768 *Triton alpestris* Laurenti
1882 *Molge alpestris* Boulenger
1918 *Triturus alpestris* Dunn

Like most members of the genus, this species is restricted to Europe, where it has, however, a quite extensive range throughout Central and north-east France, Belgium, Holland, Germany, Denmark, Switzerland, North Spain, North Italy, Austria, Yugoslavia, North Greece, and parts of Russia. It shows sufficient variation in various parts of its range to have been divided into seven subspecies.

Its common name is to some slight extent misleading; it is abundant in many Alpine regions, but it is by no means confined to them. The largest populations are mostly to be found in hilly or mountainous districts, but sizeable colonies are also to be met with in some lowland areas. In north-central Europe, for example, it is common in the hilly areas of Thuringia, the Harz, and the Deister, but also occurs in quite large numbers in the flat country round Hanover and further north, and more sporadically throughout Schleswig-Holstein and into Denmark. Although it reaches the coast of the

English Channel in Holland, Belgium, and north-east France, it is absent from the British Isles, having presumably arrived in the area after the English Channel was formed. In the Alps and Carpathians it reaches almost 10,000 ft above sea level.

Of the seven subspecies currently recognised, only one spreads as far north as Central Europe. The distribution strongly suggests that the species was divided during the ice ages into a number of disconnected groups in the three southern refuges, and that many of the present differences developed while the range of the species was thus broken up. Four of the subspecies are still limited to extremely small ranges in south-east Europe.

This is a medium-sized newt, but the size varies to some extent between the subspecies, and the females generally grow larger than the males. An average mature length for males is around $3\frac{1}{2}$ in and for females about 4 in, but occasionally much larger females are found, up to about 5 in. The head is fairly large, almost as wide as it is long, with a broad rounded snout. The body is reasonably stout, slightly flat-sided in the males and plumper in the females. The tail is usually a little less than half the total length, though in the females it tends to be a trifle longer, often reaching a full half the total length. It is laterally compressed and, especially in the females, quite deep. The end is pointed with a fairly abrupt taper. The limbs are strongly built, the digits flattened and rather stubby, particularly on the hind-limbs. The skin is finely granulated and almost velvety on land, but becomes smoother during aquatic periods. This smoothness is more visible in the males than in the females, which usually retain a slight granulation, most noticeable on the flanks.

The most evident diagnostic feature of the Alpine Newt is the uniform bright orange or deep red colour of the abdomen in both sexes. The upper surface and sides are dark grey or nearly black. During the breeding season, a bluish or purplish hue may suffuse the normally darker colour, which at that time also becomes rather lighter with more or less evidence of darker mottling. The upper colour of breeding females is particularly variable, old specimens especially often tending to be olive-greenish or brownish. The lower edge of the tail in the female is orange or yellowish. In both sexes during the breeding season, the lower flanks become light yellowish or whitish, dotted with small black spots in the female and rather larger black blotches in the male. The lower edge of this light area is bordered by a sky-blue stripe, very prominent in the male but less noticeable and sometimes absent in the female. The breeding male develops a low, continuous, smooth-edged crest, light yellow with a regular series of black marks about the same width as the yellow spaces. The black marks may either oppose each other on either side of the crest, or alternate to some degree to give the impression of a narrow zig-zag stripe when viewed from above. Young newts which have just left the water frequently have a yellow, orange, or reddish dorsal stripe, often limited to the region just behind the head. It normally disappears with age but may persist in faded form in adult females.

The habits of this newt are similar to those of other members of the genus, but in many respects it appears to be more adaptable than most. On land it is nocturnal and crepuscular, and often appears abroad quite early in the evening at the onset of dusk, before other species usually venture out. It would appear to wander about more freely than other species, and specimens can often be found far from water or under isolated stones in open fields, where other species inhabiting the same general area would rarely be met. Probably more than any other *Triturus* species it appears to enter and leave the water outside the breeding season, the impression being that if it reaches water during its wanderings it goes straight in instead of skirting the edge as other newts would do. It is certainly able to withstand considerable cold, being active at quite low temperatures and able to survive at least short periods below freezing-point. Experiment has shown that in this respect it is more hardy than either *T. cristatus* or *T. vulgaris.*

In the water, these newts are bottom-dwellers rather than free swimmers, but they are by no means choosy as to the type of water they frequent. They may be found in very small shallow pools or quite large bodies of water, as well as in slow-flowing streams. In lakes and large ponds, they do not show the tendency other species have to limit themselves to either deep or shallow water. They may be found in a few inches of water among grass roots where the verges of a pond have been temporarily flooded as well as in open deep water far out from the bank. A measurement taken in the middle of one pond where numbers were seen to rise for air showed the depth to be between 6 and 7 ft; the newts swam to the surface quite strongly and immediately descended again. The only other species seen rising from this depth was *T. cristatus*; the *T. vulgaris* and *T. helveticus* in the same pond were in shallower water nearer the bank, except for some *T. vulgaris* keeping close to the surface.

The breeding season, or at least the general movement to water preceding breeding, occurs quite early in the year, sometimes as early as February and in many areas very soon after the ice has thawed. Courtship takes place mostly during the months of March to May, though this may vary according to the locality and weather conditions. The courtship display of the male is a generalised one along the lines already described for the genus as a whole, the male keeping close to the female throughout and displaying rather less vigorously than the males of most other species. Around 150 eggs are laid by each female, mostly in April and May, and hatch out in two to four weeks according to temperature. The larvae, which superficially appear dusky grey in colour, reach a comparatively large size in proportion to the size of the adults and develop quite large and bushy external gills. They generally metamorphose some three months after hatching but frequently overwinter before metamorphosing; and there is a noticeable tendency in this newt, particularly in some subspecies, towards neoteny, whereby the larval stage persists and the creature remains permanently aquatic.

The normal food of this species consists of small crustaceans, insects and their larvae, worms, and slugs. In the water they seem to have a better sense of smell than most of the smaller newts and, in conjunction with their bottom-dwelling habits, prefer to find most of their food on or in the mud at the bottom of their pond or pool rather than hunt active or free-swimming prey. The feeding habits of the larvae are very similar to those of the tadpoles of other species. For a while after the eggs hatch, the minute larvae feed on infusoria, but as they later become larger and more mobile, they actively pursue small creatures such as water-fleas. By the time full larval size is reached, they can tackle insect larvae and small worms, or almost anything they can catch and swallow.

TRITURUS ALPESTRIS ALPESTRIS (*LAURENTI*)   ALPINE NEWT
1768 *Triton alpestris* Laurenti
1768 *Triton salamandroides* Laurenti
1923 *Triturus alpestris alpestris* Mertens

The typical form has by far the widest range of all subspecies and essentially occupies Central Europe, the other races occurring in smaller areas around the fringes of the total range. To the north, this subspecies reaches well into Denmark, and it is particularly abundant in many of the more hilly regions of Germany. It is found in Belgium, Holland, and Luxemburg, and extends into north-east France. Further south in France, it occurs in many of the eastern districts and in the French Alps, whence it continues through South France into North Italy. It apparently does not occur in the Pyrenees and a report that it has been found in Central Spain appears to require confirmation. In the east of its range, it reaches the Carpathians and parts of Poland. A considerable extension of the range in south-east Europe takes this form as far as North Greece.

TRITURUS ALPESTRIS APUANUS (*BONAPARTE*)

ITALIAN ALPINE NEWT

1839 *Triton apuanus* Bonaparte
1897 *Triton alpestris immaculatus* Dürigen
1934 *Triturus alpestris apuana* Wolterstorff
1940 *Triturus alpestris apuanus* Mertens & Müller

This subspecies is found only in a fairly limited area of North Italy, in Liguria, and north-west Tuscany. It appears to intergrade to some extent with the nominate race and specimens from some areas, such as the Genoa region, are not always easy to distinguish.

The ventral coloration in this form is a vivid deep red. The throat is covered with dark blotches and ocellations, which sometimes extend on to the ventral surface. The maximum size tends to be somewhat less than that of the main subspecies.

TRITURUS ALPESTRIS CYRENI *WOLTERSTORFF 1932*

SPANISH ALPINE NEWT

This subspecies constitutes an isolated population based on Lake Ercina, which lies at an elevation of over 3,000 ft near Covadonga in the Cantabrian Mountains of north-west Spain.

Although presumably isolated for a long time, it does not differ radically from the nominate race. The main obvious difference is in the shape of the head, which is noticeably broader and more rounded in outline.

TRITURUS ALPESTRIS LACUSNIGRI (*SELIŠKAR & PEHANI*)

BALKAN ALPINE NEWT

1935 *Triton alpestris lacusnigri* Seliškar & Pehani
1940 *Triturus alpestris lacusnigri* Mertens & Müller

Found only at Crno Jezero in the Julian Alps in north-west Yugoslavia, this is also one of the forms restricted to a very limited area.

It is distinguished by its generally darker coloration, nearly black on the upper surfaces. Although the body and tail are somewhat long and slender, the head is quite large and angular.

TRITURUS ALPESTRIS MONTENEGRINUS *RADOVANOVIČ 1951*

MONTENEGRAN ALPINE NEWT

The comparatively recent establishment of this subspecies is based on a population in Bukumirsko Lake in Montenegro which has gone a long way towards adopting a completely aquatic existence. With very few exceptions (which possibly do not survive to breed), these newts fail to metamorphose and leave the water, but are capable of breeding in the larval state. Apart from this neoteny, the adoption of an aquatic existence seems to have brought about a few minor physical changes, such as an unusual arrangement of the vomero-palatine teeth and a reduction in size of the mouth. The head is remarkably large, probably larger in proportion to the size of the body than in any other subspecies. Very little is known about its general life-history.

TRITURUS ALPESTRIA REISERI (*WERNER*)

BOSNIAN ALPINE NEWT

1902 *Molge alpestris reiseri* Werner
1928 *Triturus alpestris reiseri* Mertens & Müller

The home of this subspecies is high in the Vranika mountains in Bosnia.

It is of robust build, the head in adult specimens being particularly large and broad. Neoteny has frequently been observed, but not so consistently as in *montenegrinus*.

TRITURUS ALPESTRIS VELUCHIENSIS *WOLTERSTORFF*

GREEK ALPINE NEWT

1935 *Triturus alpestris graeca* Wolterstorff
1935 *Triturus alpestris veluchiensis* Wolterstorff

As with several other subspecies, this appears to be another example of a population left isolated at high level as the climate of South Europe became warmer. It occurs in the Veluchi Mountains of Central Greece at not less than 5,000 ft and probably up to 6,500 ft or more above sea level. Its isolation is probably not very remote in time and still depends on altitude rather than geographical distance from the main subspecies, which is probably why it is not greatly different in form. The main diagnostic feature is a tendency to have a few dark blotches on the ventral surface and for the light blue stripe on the lower flank to be as prominent in the females as in the males.

Triturus boscai (Lataste)   **Bosca's Newt**

1879 *Pelonectes boscai* Lataste
1882 *Molge boscae* Boulenger
1918 *Triturus boscai* Dunn

Yet a further example of a species which has obviously not extended its range a great deal since the end of the Ice Ages is this small newt, which is still limited in its range to the Iberian Peninsula. Even here, it is absent from the eastern and north eastern parts of the peninsula, though otherwise it is reasonably abundant in many parts of Spain and Portugal.

The species shows a preference for hilly country, and when found at lower levels is usually near to hills. This undoubtedly ties in with its preference during the breeding season for mountain streams or clear pools rather than standing or muddy waters. Temperature may be a factor in this, and perhaps the preference for cool water is one of the reasons why the species has not extended its range further.

Superficially, Bosca's Newt resembles both the Palmate Newt and the Smooth Newt, though it is smaller than the latter. The total length rarely exceeds 4 in and may be as little as 3 in for full-grown specimens. The body and limbs are fairly slender. The tail, which makes up a little more than half the total length, is laterally compressed with small crests above and below. Its extremity is rounded and in the males and many females ends in a small point, reminiscent of the tail filament of the Palmate Newt but much smaller. The head is longer than it is broad and somewhat rectangular, though the snout is moderately rounded. From behind the snout a shallow groove runs backwards across the top of the head between the eyes. The skin is smooth and there is a gular fold under the throat.

Unlike most other species in the genus, the male does not develop any kind of cutaneous adornment during the breeding season. It is nevertheless quite easy to tell the sexes apart. The general colour of the males is a fairly light yellowish-brown, while the females are a dark olive-brown. The body and tail are more or less regularly dotted with small dark spots, and in some cases a narrow yellowish dorsal stripe is present. The belly is a bright orange-yellow. This colour tends to extend along the lower edge of the tail, though in the males this extension is normally confined to a limited area near the base of the tail and is partially obscured by a series of black markings. In most specimens the belly is immaculate, but sometimes a few black spots tend to form a regular series along each side of the belly. The colours of the upper and lower surfaces are divided by a whitish or yellowish area running along the lower flank. The tiny point at the end of the tail is whitish.

The cloacal region of the male is a rounded protuberance of the normal type for the genus, but the female has a flattened cone-shaped protuberance directed backwards rather than downwards.

Being small, this newt is necessarily limited to small prey, and feeds largely on tiny free-swimming water-life. Its sense of smell does not appear to be very well developed and it probably depends largely on its eyesight to find its food. It is quite an active newt and is adept at catching small moving creatures such as water-fleas and insect larvae.

The breeding sequence follows the normal pattern for the genus. The adult newts repair to water during the spring and leave the water again around June, to spend the rest of the year on land. At least in some of the more easterly parts of its range, it breeds in streams or pools which may dry up during a particularly dry summer.

Triturus cristatus (Laurenti)   Crested Newt
1768 *Triton cristatus* Laurenti
1918 *Triturus cristatus* Dunn

There seems little doubt that this is another example of a species which was broken up during the last glaciation into a number of isolated populations, some of which have since joined up to make the present overall range quite extensive. The effects of the period of isolation are at least partly responsible for the current division of the species into subspecies, though the differentiation into highland and lowland forms may be of older origin.

The range of the species as a whole covers most of Europe and a part of west Asia. The northern subspecies (*T. c. cristatus*) has extended its range to 67° N in Scandinavia and to the extreme north of Scotland, but does not extend westward further than Central France, and in the more southerly areas of France and in the Iberian Peninsula is replaced by *Triturus marmoratus*. The same subspecies reaches well into Russia in the east of its range, while another subspecies further south reaches as far east as North Iran.

Although some subspecies are more adapted to high elevations than others, the Crested Newt is basically a lowland species, being rarely found above 3,000 ft in any part of its range, and generally at much lower levels. It might almost be regarded as a woodland species, since it is very much at home in deciduous woods though by no means confined to them. Ford (1954), referring to *T. c. cristatus*, says that it has a preference for clay soils, and this would appear to be generally true, but sizeable populations exist in many sandy, limestone, and even chalk areas. What perhaps affects the local distribution of this newt more than anything else is the right kind of water for breeding, since there is no doubt that it prefers fairly deep, weedy pools and during the daytime at least remains at greater depth than most other newts.

It is impossible to confuse the Crested Newt with any other species. It is a large newt, the males reaching a length of $5\frac{1}{2}$ to 6 in and the females $6\frac{1}{2}$ in or exceptionally even slightly more. The body is moderately slender in proportion to the size and generally round in section, though the females have somewhat the greater width. The head is almost as broad as it is long, rather flattened and well set off from the neck, with a rounded though fairly prominent snout. The tail is strongly built, slightly less than half the total length, and laterally compressed with prominent keels above and below. The limbs are long, particularly in the males, which also have longer fingers and toes than the females. Most females have a shallow dorsal groove running the length of the body.

The skin, as is indicated by the alternative name 'Warty Newt', is strongly granular, though changes in the nature of the dermis reduce this condition during the breeding season (Malcolm Smith, 1954). It is abundantly supplied with mucous glands, which results in its retaining a moist appearance even during the terrestrial stage, as opposed to the velvety appearance of many other newts at this time.

The basic coloration is somewhat variable but is generally very dark brown or black, often becoming lighter during the breeding season to show a fairly large number of black blotches dotted irregularly over the back and sides of the body and anterior tail. The sides of the head and body are thickly sprinkled with white, more prominent during the breeding season and particularly noticeable in breeding males. The belly is yellow or vermilion, blotched with black, the lighter colour extending along the lower edge of the tail in the females. The limbs are likewise marbled in the dark and light colours, extending on to the toes in regular interspacing. The underside of the head is mottled dark brown and dingy white.

Some at least of the glands in the skin can produce a secretion which appears to have irritant and probably toxic properties, and presumably deters predators (Malcolm Smith, 1954). The European Grass Snake *Natrix natrix* has often been observed to eat the Crested Newt, but just as often to reject it after seizing it, even though other species of newt are eaten readily. The introduction of a number of terrapins into a pond in England where all three British species of newt had bred for many years resulted in rapid elimination of all except the Crested Newts, which continued to maintain a breeding population. A captive American water-snake (*Natrix sipedon fasciata*) which swallowed a Crested Newt regurgitated it after a few minutes, covered with thick white slime, and died within an hour. When disturbed, the Crested Newt frequently gives off a strongly pungent smell, even at times when there is no obvious sign of glandular secretion.

During the breeding season the male develops a high dorsal crest extending from the back of the head almost to the end of the tail, except normally for a gap above the base of the tail. The crest is denticulated, strongly so on the body and less so on the tail. With the end of the breeding season, the crest is absorbed to leave only a slight ridge along the body. The adult males also have a broad white stripe running medially along each side of the tail, but fading out towards the base of the tail. This stripe is noticeable at all times but becomes much more distinct during the breeding season. Normally, the crest begins to grow and the tail-stripe to intensify in colour just before the males go into hibernation; complete development of both then takes place rapidly when the males emerge in the spring and enter the water.

Hibernation usually takes place on land, though occasionally adults enter the water in autumn and remain more or less dormant on the bottom throughout the winter (Steward, 1966). Hibernation appears, however, to be less intense in water than on the land, and Crested Newts have on more than one occasion been seen moving around under the ice. The time when the bulk of the adults enters the water in the spring varies considerably according to the locality and prevailing weather conditions. In the southern part of the British Isles, it is usually during the second half of March. They return to land about early July, some two or three weeks after the Smooth Newt leaves the water.

The courtship performance of the male is generally typical of the genus, but has some specific characteristics. He does not emulate the rapid movements of smaller species such as *T. vulgaris* and *T. helveticus*, but moves in a comparatively slow and ungainly manner, keeping close to the female and always endeavouring to place himself squarely across her path. The legs are held stiffly to hold the body off the ground, and the body is strongly arched, while the tail is curved towards the female and intermittently vibrated with considerable vigour. To human eyes, the effect is almost one of intimidation rather than display. In any case, the effect on the female is usually sufficient to persuade her to pick up the spermatophore which is eventually deposited.

Egg-laying by the female commences in April in most areas and continues for most of the time that the newts remain in the water. Each female lays some 200 to 300 eggs during the course of the breeding season, each being laid separately and folded into a leaf or stem of grass, or occasionally attached to a stick or stone. The eggs are about 2 mm in diameter, with yellowish nuclei. The larvae, which on hatching are about 8 mm long or sometimes a little more, are a light greenish-brown above and dingy white below. Many dark spots and occasionally a few light ones develop on the back and sides. The body of a well grown larva is robust, the limbs and digits are long and slender, and a smooth-edged dorsal crest runs from behind the head to the end of the tail, which tapers finely. A further crest runs along the lower edge of the tail. Metamorphosis and departure from the water take place some four months after hatching, by which time the young newts have reached a length of around 2½ to 3 in and taken on more or less the colour pattern of the adult females. Late-hatched larvae may overwinter in the water before metamorphosing. The males do not develop their crests or tail-stripes until about the third year, by which time both males and females are as a rule sexually mature and ready to breed in the following spring.

The summer and usually the winter are spent on land in most places. During the day, the newts remain under cover in thick grass or under logs or stones and emerge at night, particularly in wet weather, to forage for food. This nocturnal tendency remains when the newts are in the water, as they are inclined to remain on the bottom in fairly deep water during the day, and often move into shallow water around the edges of the pond at night. Unlike *T. vulgaris*, however, they rarely leave the water for short periods at night.

The larvae are voracious feeders and tackle almost anything moving which is small enough for them to swallow, including water-insects and insect larvae of various kinds, and small worms. The adults on land feed largely on worms, slugs, caterpillars, and the like, but the prey is always seized in the jaws and never picked up on the tongue in the way that some of the smaller newts catch tiny insects. There is one record of a Crested Newt eating a small Slowworm. The prey is usually shaken rather violently before being swallowed. In the water, a wide range of invertebrates is eaten, and to some extent this newt uses its sense of smell in the water to find food in the bottom mud. Small water-snails are often swallowed, as well as caddis-worms, which may be dragged from their case or, if small, even occasionally swallowed complete with case.

TRITURUS CRISTATUS CRISTATUS (*LAURENTI*)

NORTHERN CRESTED NEWT

1768 *Triton cristatus* Laurenti
1928 *Triturus cristatus cristatus* Mertens & Müller

This is the main subspecies, covering all the range of the species except some areas in South Europe and West Africa. It reaches 60° N in much of northern Europe and 67° N in Scandinavia, and as far south as the Alps. The east to west range is very extensive, from Central and East France to Central Russia, where its easterly boundary is not well defined but extends in some places across the Urals. In the British Isles, it has been found from Land's End to the extreme north of Scotland, but not in Ireland.

TRITURUS CRISTATUS CARNIFEX (*LAURENTI*)

ALPINE CRESTED NEWT

1768 *Triton carnifex* Laurenti
1928 *Triturus cristatus carnifex* Mertens & Müller

The range of this subspecies embraces North Italy and the Southern Alps; the Alpine regions of Austria north to Salzburg, Linz, and Vienna; and North Yugoslavia.

It tends to be slightly shorter on average than the typical form, adults normally measuring $4\frac{1}{2}$ to 6 in, though occasionally reaching a length of 7 in. It is generally more robust in build, with a broader head, than any of the other subspecies, and longer legs. The crest of the male is high and the gap between the dorsal and caudal sections is placed a little further

Page 107 (*above*) Banded Salamander *Salamandra salamandra terrestris*. Male (*below*) Head of Banded Salamander *Salamandra salamandra terrestris*

Page 108 Hybrid *Salamandra salamandra terrestris x bejarae*, showing inter-

back than in the other subspecies, behind the point of attachment of the hind-legs rather than more or less above it. The skin is finely granulated or even sometimes smooth.

The ground colour is grey, brownish, or dark olive-green with large, more or less distinct, dark grey or black spots. The white dots on the flanks are sparse or absent, but those on the sides of the head are more evident. The belly is orange or vermilion with dark grey or black blotches, and the throat brown with small white spots. The distinction between the males and females is similar to that in the typical form, except that the crest of the male is more crenulated and most females have a yellow stripe along the middle of the back.

This appears to be a particularly hardy form and even at high levels the adults may be found in the water soon after the ice disperses, in some areas as early as February. It seems probable that many overwinter in the water. The male is said not to arch his back during the courtship dance.

TRITURUS CRISTATUS DOBROGICUS (*KIRITZESCU*)

DANUBE CRESTED NEWT

1903 *Triton cristatus dobrogicus* Kiritzescu
1923 *Triton cristatus danubialis* Wolterstorff
1928 *Triturus cristatus dobrogicus* Mertens & Müller

This subspecies has a comparatively small range, in the general area of the Danube basin from a little west of Vienna to the Black Sea. It is thus a lowland form as compared with the previous subspecies, and the boundary between their respective ranges is mainly a geophysical one in this respect.

It is comparatively small, rarely much exceeding 5 in long, and very slender, with a narrow head and small weak legs. The granulations on the skin are large and coarse. The colour of the upper surfaces is brownish with small black spots. The white spots on the sides are more evident than in the Alpine Crested Newt, but less so than in the typical subspecies. The

G

belly is orange or vermilion with dark brown or black blotches, mostly very distinct. The crest of the male is strongly denticulated along the back, except that an initial short section from above the eyes on to the nape is normally quite smooth. On the tail, the crest is comparatively low and smooth.

TRITURUS CRISTATUS KARELINII (*STRAUCH*)

SOUTHERN CRESTED NEWT

1870 *Triton karelinii* Strauch
1897 *Triton cristatus karelinii* Dürigen
1928 *Triturus cristatus karelinii* Mertens & Müller

Like the Alpine Crested Newt, with which it was at one time confused, this is a highland form, found in the hilly and mountainous areas of the Caucasus and spreading east as far as the southern end of the Caspian Sea in North Iran, north as far as the Crimea, and west into Europe only as far as the eastern Balkan region.

It is the largest of the four subspecies, females sometimes reaching a length of 8 in, whereas it is exceptional for those of any of the other subspecies to exceed 7 in. Moreover, it is a robust form with a stout trunk and long well-developed legs. The head is large and broad and somewhat flattened. In proportion to the total length, the body is comparatively short, usually with 15 pre-sacral vertebrae as against the normal 16 or 17. The skin is noticeably granular, and the crest of the male of moderate height with little or no gap between the dorsal and caudal sections.

The upper parts are brownish or even greenish, usually with large, round black blotches which extend on to the orange stomach. The white spots on the sides are sparse or absent, but tend to increase in numbers on the sides of the head. The throat is brownish with sometimes a few dark blotches and some white dots. This subspecies sometimes has a bluish sheen, especially over the white flash on the male's tail and on the dark blotches of the flanks and stomach.

Triturus helveticus (Razoumowsky) **Palmate Newt**
1789 *Lacerta helvetica* Razoumowsky
1799 *Salamandra palmata* Schneider
1800 *Salamandra palmipes* Latreille
1918 *Triturus helveticus* Dunn

The range of this newt is confined to Western Europe, extending eastwards only approximately as far as a line drawn southwards from Hamburg in Germany. Presumably its ice-age refuge was in the north of the Iberian Peninsula, where one of the two subspecies still occupies a limited area.

Its general similarity in appearance and habits to the Smooth Newt, and the fact that their ranges overlap over a large area, frequently cause the two species to be confused, and it is not easy to understand how they can so often exist side by side in the same areas and breed in the same pools without noticeably competing with each other. The main obvious difference in their choice of habitat is that the Palmate Newt favours hilly or mountainous regions and is less at home at low levels than the Smooth Newt, so that throughout the general area occupied by both species it is possible in some districts to find only the Palmate Newt and in others only the Smooth Newt, with intervening zones where both exist in varying proportions. Soil may also be a factor, as the Palmate Newt is generally more often found on sandy, peaty, or limestone soils than on clay or alluvium. Its preference for high altitudes is more noticeable in the south of its range, where in places it ascends to almost 6,000 ft, but even in the more northerly parts of its range it can be found up to almost 3,000 ft above sea level.

With the possible exception of Bosca's Newt, this is the smallest of the European urodeles. The average total length of full-grown males is about 3 in and of females just slightly more, but exceptional specimens may reach nearly 4 in. The head is longer than it is broad, with a fairly broad snout which is slightly more rounded in the females than in the males. The body is slender (though females may be quite plump during the breeding season) and the tail slightly longer than the snout-vent length. The skin is so finely granulated as to appear superficially smooth.

Sexual dimorphism is pronounced. The female greatly resembles the female of the Smooth Newt, being olive-green or light brown above, sometimes speckled or marbled with dark green. In some specimens, the darker markings may fuse to form a dorso-lateral line. The male is beautifully marked with dark green speckles or marbling on an olive-green ground, and the longitudinally central section on each side of the tail is light brown or olive, edged above and below with a row of prominent dark spots. In both sexes, the belly is pale orange or yellow, uniform or spotted with brown, and the throat is a clear white or pale pink. A dark line on each side of the head runs through the golden iris of the eye. During the breeding season, the male develops a low smooth crest, complete black webs on the hind-feet, and a short filament extending from the end of the otherwise abruptly truncated tail-tip. In addition, a glandular pad running the whole length of the back from the neck to the base of the tail increases in size to form a prominently angular ridge. A similar gland on the female develops to a lesser and hardly noticeable degree.

The breeding cycle is similar to that of most other newts in the genus, the adults being found in water in the spring and usually spending most of the rest of the year on land. Almost any body of water may be chosen, from small pools to large ponds or slow-moving brooks. Shallow water is obviously preferred, and in larger bodies of water they are more likely to be found in shallow water near the bank than in deeper water in the middle. A shelving edge with a muddy bottom and abundant vegetation constitutes an ideal situation. Courtship usually takes place in such shallow areas and involves a vigorous display on the part of the male, who places himself repeatedly in the path of the female and curves his whole body towards her, lashing his tail rapidly. Some 300 to 400 eggs are laid by the female and attached to water-plants singly. The nucleus is yellow-brown, darker above than below. On hatching, the larvae are about 8 mm long and normally metamorphose at a length of about 1 in. They resemble the larvae of the Smooth Newt but may usually be distinguished by examining the eyes and nostrils: in the Palmate Newt, the distance between nostril and eye is less than the diameter of the eye, whereas in the Smooth Newt the two measurements are roughly the same.

Small worms and insects are the main food. In the water, prey is seized in the jaws or snapped up in the mouth; on land, larger items such as worms and caterpillars are seized in the jaws; but probably the bulk of the food consists of tiny insects such as greenfly, which are picked up on the tip of the tongue and carried back into the mouth.

TRITURUS HELVETICUS HELVETICUS (*RAZOUMOWSKY*)

PALMATE NEWT

1789 *Lacerta helvetica* Razoumowsky
1928 *Triturus helveticus helveticus* Mertens & Müller

The use of trinomials for this species is hardly justified, as it is only in the south-west corner of its range that slight differences are apparent from the normal characteristics. Otherwise, over the whole of its range, it is virtually impossible to distinguish any variation.

TRITURUS HELVETICUS SEQUEIRAI (*WOLTERSTORFF*)

IBERIAN PALMATE NEWT

1905 *Triton palmatus sequeirai* Wolterstorff
1928 *Triturus helveticus sequeirai* Mertens & Müller

In North Portugal and north-west Spain, the Palmate Newt is slightly smaller than elsewhere, the males, particularly, rarely exceeding $2\frac{1}{2}$ in and the females only occasionally reaching 3 in. The dorsal surface is somewhat yellowish and lighter than in the nominate race. On the strength of these differences Wolterstorff specified the populations in this area as a separate form, and they have been accepted as such ever since, though the differences are hardly sufficient to warrant this separate status.

Triturus marmoratus (Latreille)   **Marbled Newt**
1800 *Salamandra marmorata* Latreille
1918 *Triturus marmoratus* Dunn

Closely related though it is to *Triturus cristatus*, the Marbled Newt presumably broke off from the common stock long before the Crested Newt became subdivided into its present subspecies. Nevertheless, its present existence as a separate species almost certainly results from isolation during one or other of the glacial periods, and even now the two species are still able to hybridise to some extent, such hybridisation taking place in the wild on occasion in a strip of country across North and Central France where the two ranges overlap. These hybrids have in the past been accorded unwarranted specific status, as *Triton blasii* and *Triton trouessarti* respectively for those with a Crested Newt father and those with a Marbled Newt father.

The refuge of the species during the last glacial period was no doubt entirely south of the Pyrenees, but the species has subsequently spread further north. The present range therefore covers not only virtually the whole of Spain and Portugal, but most of France west of the Rhône valley (as well as a strip further east along the Mediterranean coast) and south-west of a line running approximately through Rouen, Paris, and Troyes. In many perimeter areas, such as the Channel coast and the Auvergne, it is by no means common, but is far more plentiful in south-west France and in the Atlantic coastal areas as far north as South Brittany. Reports of this newt from Switzerland are based on misidentification of the Alpine Newt, large females of which may occasionally develop a greenish marbled appearance reminiscent of the Marbled Newt; the latter is not found anywhere in Switzerland.

TRITURUS MARMORATUS MARMORATUS (*LATREILLE*)

MARBLED NEWT

1800 *Salamandra marmorata* Latreille
1828 *Salamandra variegata* Bory
1839 *Salamandra elegans* Lesson
1841 *Triton marmoratus* Dumeril & Bibron
1928 *Triturus marmoratus marmoratus* Mertens & Müller

This main subspecies has the same range as the whole of the species except for the area in the southern part of the Iberian Peninsula occupied by the subspecies *pygmaeus* (see p 117).

Throughout its area, the Marbled Newt is largely confined to lower altitudes, and is not often found more than about 1,200 ft above sea level. Where it has penetrated into generally high-lying regions such as the Central Massif of France, it has done so along the valleys. It is not particularly choosy about soil conditions, and thrives well in clay quarries in South France, sandy areas in West France and among the limestone hills of north-east Spain. In general, however, it is more particular in its choice of a breeding site. Running water is normally avoided and it prefers small but reasonably deep ponds, pools, and ditches, especially where there is an abundance of water-vegetation.

In size and shape, the Marbled Newt resembles the Crested Newt. It normally reaches a length of 5 to $5\frac{1}{2}$ in, and occasionally exceeds 6 in. The body is sub-cylindrical in section and moderately slender, though increasing slightly in diameter posteriorly. The head is a little broader than it is long, the eyes large and prominent, and the snout fairly broad, short, and rounded, its rather truncated appearance being enhanced by a downward slope of the upper surface from the eyes to the forward-placed nostrils. The length of the tail is roughly equal to the snout-vent length, sometimes a little more, and the tail is strongly compressed laterally. The limbs and digits are fairly long and slender, particularly in the male.

The skin is granular (less so on the under surface) and furnished with many pores on the head and around the base of each limb, but the mottled coloration tends to mask the effect of these granulations so that from a superficial examination the skin appears fairly smooth. The crest of the male is high and more or less smooth-edged with a gap between the dorsal and caudal sections. Outside the breeding season, the crest diminishes considerably but a vestige usually remains evident. Low keels are present along the lower edge of the tail in the male and both upper and lower edges in the female. The latter has a shallow vertebral groove running the length of the body.

The Marbled Newt is undoubtedly the most attractively coloured of all the members of the genus *Triturus*. The basic colour is green, thickly blotched or marbled with black. The green may vary from light yellow-green to a dark olive-green, but is usually quite vivid, possibly more so when the newts are on land than when they are in the water. The dark blotches are larger in the male than in the female, and sometimes fuse on the lower flank to form a continuous line. On the digits, the black markings form regular cross-bands as in the Crested Newt. The under surface is grey to dark brown, often spotted with black and white. Juveniles and females have a narrow vertebral stripe, orange-red in the young and usually somewhat paler in adult females. During the breeding season, the crest of the male is banded with alternate black and dull white vertical bars, and a silvery stripe along each side of the tail becomes more prominent.

Breeding starts in the spring, when the adults repair to water, mostly small pools and ponds. Courtship display by the male is similar to that of the Crested Newt, including the arching of the back. The first eggs are laid in March to May, according to locality and weather, and altogether a total of some 200 or 300 or more eggs are laid singly and attached to water-plants. The adults often stay in the water until well into the summer, and cases have been reported of adults in the water and breeding in the autumn. The eggs have a pale green nucleus and hatch in two or three weeks, according to temperature. The larvae are reddish-brown, speckled with dark brown, and have a greenish sheen. Metamorphosis takes place in about three months.

When on land, the newts are nocturnal, hiding away by day and coming out at dusk or later to search for food. Their habits at this time, including choice of food, correspond closely to those of the Crested Newt. The Marbled Newt tends, however, to be more aquatic than the Crested Newt and may enter the water occasionally throughout the year when not hibernating.

The hybrids resulting from *marmoratus* × *cristatus* crosses generally resemble the Marbled Newt in the coloration of the upper surfaces and the Crested Newt in the coloration of the under surface. Where the two species overlap, they generally breed true and the number of hybrids remains limited. The precise reason for this is not altogether clear, but it seems probable that the hybrids can breed back into one or other of the parent species but further breeding between hybrids results in sterile offspring.

TRITURUS MARMORATUS PYGMAEUS (*WOLTERSTORFF*)

SOUTHERN MARBLED NEWT

1905 *Triton marmoratus pygmaea* Wolterstorff
1928 *Triturus marmoratus pygmaeus* Mertens & Müller

Wolterstorff established this form on the basis of specimens from Cadiz which were generally smaller than the typical form. It is now known that over an area in the southern parts of the Iberian Peninsula the Marbled Newt reaches a length of only around $3\frac{1}{2}$ to 4 in (some females slightly more), but the precise range of this form has not yet been determined. In all other respects the two forms are identical, except for minor differences in colour and it is possible that this may prove to be a case of a graduated cline rather than a sharp division between the two forms. The validity of the subspecies is therefore not altogether certain.

Triturus montandoni (Boulenger)   Carpathian Newt
1880 *Triton montandoni* Boulenger
1918 *Triturus montandoni* Dunn

The range of this species is smaller than that of any other in the genus and it is the only one which does not anywhere reach the Mediterranean, or for that matter any sea coast of Europe. It is found only in Central Europe in the Carpathians, the Tatra Mountains, and the mountains around the upper reaches of the River Oder in Moravia. It was introduced some years ago into an area in Bavaria and established itself for a period, but has now possibly died out there. In exactly what region the species survived the ice ages is difficult to decide, but probably it has moved to its present mountainous habitat fairly recently as the climate of Europe became warmer, and has abandoned whatever more sheltered refuge sufficed to tide it over the last glacial epoch. The most obvious possibility is that this refuge was in the Danube basin. The impression that the species only just managed to get through the last glacial period rests not only on the present limited distribution but also on the rather limited altitude range it seems able to tolerate. While on the one hand it is seldom found outside the foothills of the mountain districts which constitute its range, it is on the other hand not often found above about 2,500 ft except in the Tatra, where it is reported to be fairly abundant up to about 3,000 ft. The upper altitude limit may be correlated with the upper limit of deciduous woodlands.

From its general appearance the Carpathian Newt would appear to have its closest affinities with the Palmate Newt, though it has also many points of resemblance to the Alpine Newt and, particularly as far as the females are concerned, to the Smooth Newt. Possibly it became split off from the original stock of the Palmate Newt during a glacial period, and the ranges of the two species have remained separate ever since. Its present range is entirely contained within those of the Alpine Newt and the Smooth Newt, and it is said to interbreed with the latter in the wild on occasion.

The total length of adult specimens varies between about 3 and 4 in, males being smaller than females. The head is broad and the snout short. Three shallow grooves run longitudinally along the top of the head from the snout backwards between the eyes. The body is moderately slender. The tail is slightly less than or occasionally equals half the total length and is laterally compressed, not very high, and tapers to a fine point. The skin is finely granulated, often appearing superficially quite smooth. In addition to the larger size of the females, other differences make it quite easy to distinguish the sexes, especially during the breeding season. At this time, the male develops a very low smooth-edged cutaneous crest along the vertebral line from just behind the head almost to the end of the tail. Two further ridges of skin develop dorsolaterally along the body only, running parallel to the vertebral crest. A short filament also grows out of the end of the tail, similar to that of the male Palmate Newt, though the end of the tail proper is not truncated. The coloration of the male is also reminiscent of that of the male Palmate Newt, the upper parts being light sandy yellow to olive-brown or greyish, and variously marbled or spotted with darker markings. The belly is orange-red in the middle, grading into yellow on the lower flanks, usually with a few small black dots scattered along the yellow portion. The central orange colour continues along the lower edge of the tail, but is broken by a series of blue-edged black marks. The female, on the other hand, much more resembles the Smooth Newt in build and general appearance. The dorsal skin-crests are missing, as also are the black dots on the lower flanks, and the orange lower edge of the tail is unbroken but bordered above by a series of dark markings, which may fuse to form a dark streak. The dark markings on the upper surface of the body likewise tend to fuse and form longitudinal stripes, the most prominent normally being a pair of irregular dorsolateral stripes, continuing less prominently on the tail.

The adults of this species are normally found in woodland pools and sometimes in slow-running sections of mountain streams, from March to June, when they leave the water and remain on land for the rest of the summer. They have been reported to enter the water again in autumn and hibernate in the bottom mud, but it is not certain whether this is their invariable practice or whether many of them hibernate on land as apparently sub-adults do.

The brownish eggs are laid singly, but less care is taken than by most *Triturus* species to wrap them individually in leaves, and often a number are laid in the same place and attached loosely to water-plants. Development of the larvae follows the normal pattern, and metamorphosis in most cases takes place in late summer.

The preferred food seems to consist mainly of small insects.

Triturus vittatus (Jenyns)   Banded Newt

1835 *Triton vittatus* Jenyns
1936 *Triturus vittatus* Terentjev & Černov

Like *Hynobius keyserlingi*, this species only just manages to get into the European list. Basically, it is a West African species, being found in northern Asia Minor as far south as Syria and Israel, and overlapping the European border only in the West Caucasus. It is therefore quite remarkable that this newt was first described in England, and it was for a while regarded as part of the English fauna. The original description by Gray, followed by that of Jenyns, was based on a specimen in the British Museum which was thought to have been found in England, probably in the London area, but which is now assumed to have been labelled with the wrong country of origin. To add to the confusion, Bell (1839) seems to have been convinced that it was only a variety of the Palmate Newt. Whatever the circumstances of the case, and to the disappointment of British herpetologists for more than a century, no further specimens of 'Gray's Banded Newt' have been found in this country, and it is now generally accepted that the specimen originally came from abroad.

Only one subspecies is found in the European part of the range, and therefore only this subspecies will be considered here.

TRITURUS VITTATUS OPHRYTICUS (*BERTHOLD*)   BANDED NEWT
1846 *Triton ophryticus* Berthold
1936 *Triturus vittatus ophryticus* Terentjev & Černov

This subspecies is found in the general area of the Caucasus, on both sides of the intercontinental boundary, and extends south into the northern part of Asia Minor, though the southern boundary of its range has still to be defined accurately.

It is more or less a montane form, rarely found below 2,500 ft and ascending to much greater heights, possibly even to 10,000 ft in a few places. It likes clear mountain lakes and pools, or streams where the current is not too fast-flowing. Olexa and Kral (1963) described finding this subspecies in the area of Sotschi at the foot of the West Caucasus. This was a limestone area, wooded with yew, beech, and oak. The newts were found singly or in pairs in small shallow pools in a deep rocky valley. The water was cold and devoid of vegetation.

Full-grown adults measure from 5 to $5\frac{1}{2}$ in, occasionally slightly more. The head is large and depressed, longer than it is broad though with a rather short snout. The trunk is sub-cylindrical in section and comparatively slender, especially in the males. The tail is fairly slender and measures about half the total length. The limbs are also fairly long and slender, with long digits. The skin is finely granulated but becomes smoother in the aquatic period.

The normal ground colour of this species is olive-green above and yellow to vermilion below. What really distinguishes the species, and gives it its common name, is the silvery white band, edged above and below with black, running along the lower flank and fading out gradually on the side of the tail. The throat and anterior abdomen are blotched with dark grey, and occasionally a series of faint blotches is present along each outside edge of the belly.

During the breeding season, the upper ground colour of the male becomes more vivid and reveals a large number of irregular dark spots. At the same time, it develops a high dorsal crest, resembling that of the Crested Newt in that it is strongly denticulated along the back (less so on the tail), and has a gap above the base of the tail. A series of vertical dark bars on the crest is, however, more reminiscent of the Marbled Newt, though the bars are narrower and more numerous.

Breeding takes place in early spring and follows the general pattern for the genus. The courtship dance of the male is likewise similar to that of most other species but the male is reported to shake his head up and down in addition to vibrating the tail. The legs are held stiff during courtship, so that the male appears to be balancing on the tips of the fingers and toes, which are more elongated than those of the female.

Triturus vulgaris (Linnaeus)   **Smooth Newt**
1758 *Lacerta vulgaris* Linnaeus
1758 *Lacerta palustris* Linnaeus
1768 *Triton palustris* Laurenti
1882 *Molge vulgaris* Boulenger
1918 *Triturus vulgaris* Dunn

This is the widest ranging of all European tailed amphibians, reaching further north than any other, and is the commonest species in most parts of its range. The distribution of its subspecies can only be explained on the assumption that it survived the last glacial period in several pockets in Italy and the Balkan area. The typical subspecies probably hung on in South or south-east Europe and must have spread out comparatively rapidly to reach the British Isles (including Ireland), well north in Sweden, and a long way east into West Asia. Other subspecies occupy smaller areas in Italy and the Balkans but none is found in the Iberian Peninsula, though *Triturus boscai* there seems closely related.

It is certainly a most adaptable species. Size, colour, and pattern vary considerably over the total range, and it occupies many different types of habitat. Wooded and open areas, mountains and plains, all have their populations of the Smooth Newt, and almost any kind of standing water, from temporary pools to the margins of lakes, can serve for breeding. Particularly in the more northern parts of its range, however, it may generally be considered a lowland species, found in many places in the same ponds as the Palmate Newt, but often handing over to the latter at higher levels and replacing it completely at lower levels.

Adults are generally around $2\frac{1}{2}$ to 3 in long, but often more, and even in a local breeding population the size range for either sex can be quite considerable. The build is normally fairly slender, though old females sometimes become quite plump. The laterally compressed tail constitutes slightly more than half the total length and terminates in a fine point. The top of the head is grooved longitudinally as a result of two bony ridges running from the rear of the head to join over the snout. Outside the breeding season, the skin is velvety in appearance, but shortly after the newts enter the water in the spring their skins become noticeably smoother, particularly in the males.

During the breeding season the male acquires a high vertebral crest running from the rear of the head almost to the tip of the tail, with a further crest along the lower edge of the tail, and narrow fringes of skin develop on the toes. In most subspecies the upper crest is notched or undulated. A very low smooth-edged dorsal crest is evident in the female at all times.

Both sexes repair to the water in early spring, the males first. In his courtship display the male is vigorous, approaching the female rapidly and taking up a position facing her a little from one side (Fig 5). The tail is bent almost double at about a third

Fig 5   Courtship position in *Triturus vulgaris*
(male on right)

its length from the base so that the tip is held close to the flank, and the end is vibrated rapidly. The female lays some 200 to 300 or more eggs, each separately and carefully wrapped in the leaf of a water-plant or in a doubled-over blade of grass, or occasionally on sticks and stones if no vegetation is available. Hatching takes place two to three weeks after the eggs are laid. Newly hatched tadpoles are about 6 mm in length and take some three to four months to reach the full larval size of about $1\frac{1}{2}$ in. Partly-grown tadpoles are usually light olive-brown above, more or less speckled with minute dark spots, and sometimes with a row of yellowish spots running dorso-laterally along each side of the back and on to the base of the

Page 125 (*above*) Alpine Newt *Triturus a. alpestris*. Male
(*below*) Northern Crested Newt *Triturus c. cristatus*. Male

tail. The underparts are immaculate yellowish or cream. Shortly before metamorphosis, the general colour darkens and a pattern emerges much like that of the adult female.

The larvae are at all stages difficult to distinguish from those of the Palmate Newt, though the position of the nostrils often helps towards a decision. The distance between the nostril and eye on each side in the Palmate Newt is less than the horizontal diameter of the eye, whereas in the Smooth Newt the two measurements are about the same. The larvae of the Smooth Newt can often be distinguished from the larvae of other *Triturus* species by the shape of the end of the tail, which is evenly tapered to a point without any filamental process. (Crested Newt and Alpine Newt larvae both have a small filament, the tail of the former having an invert taper and that of the latter having wide upper and lower crests tapering abruptly to a spatulate end.)

The adults leave the water in early summer (late June or early July in South England) and the first young complete metamorphosis and leave the water soon after; those hatched later or taking longer to develop remain in the larval state until much later in the year and it is common for those which have not completed their larval growth by the onset of cold weather to overwinter as larvae and metamorphose the following spring. The adults remain on land for the rest of the year, or in rare cases may re-enter the water in autumn to hibernate in the bottom mud. The young grow slowly and reach maturity after three to four years on land.

This is a more active species than most others. On land, it wanders quite considerable distances, and where more than one species occupies a given area in its range, it is often the first to colonise newly formed bodies of water. In the water the males are especially active and free-swimming. While the Crested and Alpine Newts, for example, find their food mainly on the bottom and depend to a considerable extent on their sense of smell to detect it, the Smooth Newt relies more on its

H

eyesight and frequently 'hawks' after small insects in mid-water or at the surface. The females keep more to cover among vegetation, but likewise spend much of their time at the surface rather than at the bottom. At night, both sexes may leave the water for a few hours and wander around the edges of their pond. The changeover to normal out-of-water breathing is accompanied by a few 'popping' noises, and if a pond containing a large population of these newts is visited shortly after dark on a fairly warm night, it is possible to hear these 'pops' coming from all along the edge of the pond. (Some water-snails make a rather similar noise when breathing at the surface.)

Food out of water consists of small soft-bodied insects such as greenfly, which are picked up on the tip of the tongue, and small caterpillars, worms, and slugs, which are seized in the jaws. In the water, small worms and the like are seized and tiny water-insects snapped up. Small frog tadpoles are also readily eaten, and Woollacott (1963) described how the Smooth Newt feeds on the eggs of the Common Frog *Rana temporaria*, as well as on its own eggs and tadpoles.

The Smooth Newt has many predators—several species of snake in various parts of its range, particularly the Grass Snake *Natrix natrix*, the Viperine Snake *N. maura*, and the Dice Snake *N. tessellata*, and probably by most fish-eating birds and some mammals. Certain carnivorous water-beetles attack the tadpoles, and a few larger ones could probably kill the adults. Litton (1962) recorded a case of Smooth Newts being attacked by leeches.

TRITURUS VULGARIS VULGARIS (*LINNAEUS*)   SMOOTH NEWT
1758 *Lacerta vulgaris* Linnaeus
1882 *Molge vulgaris* Boulenger
1928 *Triturus vulgaris vulgaris* Mertens & Müller

This might almost be called the Northern Smooth Newt, since it occupies most of the northern range of the species. The southern boundary of its range in Western Europe runs across

Central France to the Northern Alps, and only in southeastern Europe does it project south in a wedge between the Central Balkans and the Black Sea as far as Istanbul and into Asia Minor. The precise area of distribution in Asia Minor has not yet been properly defined, but seems to extend along the southern edge of the Black Sea to the Caucasus (Bodenheimer, 1944), where it probably joins up with the area occupied by *T. v. lantzi.* The northern boundary of the subspecies extends as far as the species ranges, except for the limited area in which *T. v. borealis* is found. In many parts of Central Europe in particular, it is by far the commonest newt, and populations in some places reach very high numbers.

The general description is as given above for the species, with slight local variation in colour and pattern. In the Deister area in West Germany, for example, the top of the head in breeding males is noticeably lighter than the rest of the body.

TRITURUS VULGARIS AMPELENSIS *FUHN & FREYTAG 1952*
RUMANIAN SMOOTH NEWT

The comparatively limited range of this subspecies lies in Rumania, in the western parts of the high plateau of Transylvania and extending east as far as the valleys of the Somes and Mureshi rivers.

Subspecific differences are mainly morphological ones affecting breeding males. The crest is much lower than in the nominate subspecies and mainly smooth-edged. A dorsolateral ridge is prominent on each side of the upper body. The end of the tail tapers in the normal way with the addition at the end of a filamental process. The cutaneous fringes on the toes are more strongly developed than in other subspecies.

TRITURUS VULGARIS BOREALIS *KAURI 1959*
NORTH SWEDISH SMOOTH NEWT

Kauri's decision that the Smooth Newt in North Sweden can be given subspecific status is based on small but consistent differences, and this is therefore an apparent case of a subspecies arising after the spread of the species from its Ice Age range. Living as it does further north than any other *Triturus* form, there is little doubt that the considerable differences in climate and habitat have favoured genetic changes, which are reflected to some extent in the external appearance.

The subspecies is found only in Sweden, taking over from *T. v. vulgaris* at 61° 30″ N and extending almost to 63° N.

The main obvious difference is in the pattern, both males and females being more or less heavily speckled, the specks frequently fusing to form large spots. In the males, which on average are rather smaller than the females, the crest is poorly developed during the breeding season, as is the comparatively small cloacal protuberance.

TRITURUS VULGARIS DALMATICUS (*KOLOMBATOVIC*)

DALMATIAN SMOOTH NEWT

1907 *Triton vulgaris dalmatica* Kolombatovic
1908 *Triton vulgaris graeca* variety *tomasinii* Wolterstorff
1940 *Triturus vulgaris tomasinii* Mertens & Müller
1960 *Triturus vulgaris dalmaticus* Mertens & Wermuth

This is again a subspecies with a rather compact range, being confined to Southern Dalmatia, Montenegro, and Hercegovina in South Yugoslavia.

The crest in breeding males remains poorly developed and smooth-edged, though the dorsolateral ridges are quite prominent. The end of the tail is truncated with a well developed filamental process. The colour along the lower edge of the tail is immaculate, lacking the spots found in most other subspecies. Females are easily identifiable by the presence of pronounced dark blotches on the upper surface.

TRITURUS VULGARIS GRAECUS (*WOLTERSTORFF*)

GREEK SMOOTH NEWT

1905 *Triton vulgaris graeca* Wolterstorff

1928 *Triturus vulgaris graecus* Mertens & Müller

The range of this subspecies covers Greece and Macedonia, as well as many of the Ionian Islands including Corfu. It is obviously closely related to the previous subspecies and in some respects even more resembles the Palmate Newt. In size it is well below the average for the species, rarely exceeding 3 in and often less. The crest is low and smooth-edged on the male, and the very prominent dorsolateral ridges give the body almost a square section. The end of the tail is truncated with a filament. The similarity to *dalmaticus* extends to the colour and pattern, though in this subspecies they are less obtrusive, the coloration being less vivid and the blotches on the female being smaller. In most cases the colour along the lower edge of the tail is immaculate, though sometimes broken by a few dark spots.

TRITURUS VULGARIS ITALICUS (*PERACCA*)

SOUTH ITALIAN SMOOTH NEWT

1898 *Molge italica* Peracca

1928 *Triturus italicus* Mertens & Müller

1960 *Triturus vulgaris italicus* Mertens & Wermuth

So different in appearance is this subspecies from all others that it was first described, and was for a long time afterwards regarded, as a separate species. It is difficult to say whether this 'apartness' arises from a long period of comparative isolation in Central and South Italy, or whether differences in habitat, particularly a warmer climate, have led to more rapid evolutionary changes in this area. The latter possibility is supported by the fact that it is quite a small form, the females reaching a maximum total length of $3\frac{1}{4}$ in and the males ranging from 2 to $2\frac{1}{2}$ in or occasionally a little more. It is noticeable that several southern subspecies among the European newts, such as *Triturus vulgaris schreiberi*, *Triturus helveticus sequeirai*, and *Triturus marmoratus pygmaeus*, are dwarf forms, and this has been attributed to the tendency for ponds and swamps to dry out during the hot season, allowing the larvae a shorter time to complete their growth and thus leading to selection of a smaller adult size. As this subspecies is found only at comparatively low levels, from sea level up to not more than about 8,000 ft, the effect of the hot season is all the greater. Breeding normally takes place in shallow bodies of water, such as ditches, pools, and coastal swamps.

The head is broader than in its nearest neighbour *T. v. meridionalis*, and the male completely lacks a dorsal crest but has a fairly deep groove running along the middle of the back. Dorsolateral ridges develop in breeding males. The tail, which makes up about one third of the total length, is quite low in both sexes, with weak keels above and below and a short filament on the abruptly rounded end. In the male as in the female, no membranes develop on the toes during the breeding season.

The colour pattern is rather striking. The males are greenish brown or olive-brown above, with irregularly scattered dark brown spots. The flanks are metallic yellow with dark brown or blue-grey blotches, which become larger and more blackish on the tail. An indistinct greyish yellow or whitish line is often present along the upper flank. The underside is vivid yellow with fairly large, round black spots, either irregularly distributed or forming a row along each side of the abdomen, while the darker yellow throat may have a few black spots. In the female, the ground colour is olive-brown, and a dorsolateral row of black dots or small blotches in some cases runs together to form a wavy dark line. During the breeding season, both sexes develop a yellow patch just above and behind the eye.

TRITURUS VULGARIS LANTZI *WOLTERSTORFF 1914*

CAUCASIAN SMOOTH NEWT

This subspecies is limited to a fairly small area in the northwestern Caucasus. It is also a rather small form in which the adults average slightly less than 3 in and rarely exceed $3\frac{1}{4}$ in.

The subspecific differences are mainly apparent in the breeding males, which have a series of dark vertical bars along the dorsal crest, little trace of dorsolateral ridges, and a gradually tapering tail ending in a fairly prominent filament.

TRITURUS VULGARIS MERIDIONALIS (*BOULENGER*)
SOUTHERN SMOOTH NEWT

1882 *Molge vulgaris meridionalis* Boulenger
1905 *Molge vulgaris kapelana* Mehely
1918 *Molge vulgaris boulengeri* Dunn
1940 *Triturus vulgaris meridionalis* Mertens & Müller

The usual common name for this subspecies is hardly diagnostic and a better one might be the North Italian Smooth Newt, since the bulk of its range falls within North and Central Italy, in addition to which it overlaps into the Tessin district of South Switzerland and into the north-western corner of Yugoslavia. Although much of this area is hilly or even mountainous, this subspecies is mainly a lowland-dweller, becoming rarer at higher levels and disappearing at around 3,000 ft above sea level.

Small bodies of water such as pools, ponds, and ditches are generally chosen as breeding sites, particularly those in a sunny position with abundant vegetation.

It is a form of moderate size, males reaching about $2\frac{3}{4}$ in and females about $3\frac{1}{2}$ in, but rather thicker in the body than the typical subspecies. In general appearance, it has some characteristics resembling those of the Palmate Newt, though less so than *dalmaticus* or *graecus*. The head is comparatively broad between the eyes, though the snout is narrow. The tail is slightly more than half the total length and ends in a fairly long filament, though otherwise tapering and not truncated. The skin is smooth or only finely granulated. During the breeding season, the male develops a crest which is moderately high above the posterior body and much of the tail, but quite low above the neck region and anterior body. This crest has no denticulations, the edge being either smooth or at the most slightly wavy. The lower tail crest is well developed at this time, as are the dorsolateral ridges.

The coloration and pattern of breeding males are similar to those of the subspecies *vulgaris*, though the background colour is normally lighter and the dark spots, which on the upper surface may be either sparse or quite numerous, are smaller. The coloration of the females is not greatly different from that of *vulgaris*.

TRITURUS VULGARIS SCHREIBERI (*WOLTERSTORFF*)

SCHREIBER'S SMOOTH NEWT

1914 *Triton vulgaris schreiberi* Wolterstorff
1940 *Triturus vulgaris schreiberi* Mertens & Müller

This race has an insignificant range, being found only in a small area of West Yugoslavia close to Bokanjacko Blato, near Zaro in Dalmatia.

Like many of the subspecies which are restricted to the southern part of the species range, it is a dwarf form, averaging a total length for adults of 2 to 2½ in and exceptionally reaching 3 in. The dorsal crest in the breeding male is low.

CHAPTER 5

The Family Plethodontidae

WITH this family, we come to a very different kind of newt from the hynobiids and salamandrids. It is for one thing basically a New World family, being strongly represented in large areas of North, Central, and South America by quite a number of different genera and species. In Europe, it is represented by only one genus, with a number of forms which for a long time were regarded as representing at least two separate species, but all of which are now considered to be subspecies of a single species. Noble (1931) expressed the view that the family arose in the New World from a salamandrid stock, and it is to be presumed that at one time it was more widely distributed in Europe. Now, however, it is limited in the Old World to a comparatively small area in North-Central Italy, extreme south-east France and Sardinia.

The most important distinction between the plethodontids and the other newts is that they are virtually lungless, respiration taking place partly through the skin and partly through a vascularised area in the throat. Up-and-down movements of the floor of the mouth serve to pump air into the throat, in the same way that in most other amphibians such movements are used to pump air into the lungs.

The increased reliance on cutaneous respiration is probably one of the reasons why the plethodontids prefer damp habitats, though the nature of these varies considerably among the various genera from forest floors and stream banks to caves, while some forms even live an arboreal life in rain forests. Habitat has no doubt been a factor in the evolution in breeding habits which has obviously taken place within the family. Some species lay their eggs in water, where they hatch into normal larvae. Some lay them in damp earth or below stones or logs close to water, into which the larvae find their way in due course. Certain of the more terrestrial species lay their eggs in underground chambers, rotten logs, or caves, and the young metamorphose within the egg before hatching.

The family is represented in Europe by the genus *Hydromantes*.

GENUS *HYDROMANTES GISTEL* 1848

The smaller genus *Hydromantes* and the closely related larger genus *Bolitoglossa* are the only plethodontid genera with species both within and outside North America, which to quote Noble (1931) 'speaks well of their travelling ability'. Whereas, however, *Bolitoglossa* is found only in the New World, though on both sides of the Isthmus of Panama, *Hydromantes* has in addition to three species in California also one species in South Europe, which not only suggests travelling ability but also that the present distribution of the species is a mere remnant of a formerly much wider one.

All four species in the genus are found in rocky limestone areas (or in granite areas in some parts of the Sierra Nevada Mountains in California), where they are found sufficiently often in caves to be known generally as 'cave salamanders'. They are superficially ungeneralised salamanders of small to moderate size, secretive and nocturnal, and entirely terrestrial in habit. A specialisation not found in most other plethodontids is the extremely protrusible tongue, furnished at the tip with a circular disc. The toes are blunt and less than half-webbed, and the tail blunt and cylindrical, often carried free of the ground and moved from side to side in synchronisation with locomotion to give the appearance of a rather lumbering walk. Little is known about the life-history of even the commoner species, but it seems fairly certain that they all lay fertilised eggs on land, from which the young emerge in the metamorphosed form.

Hydromantes genei (Temminck & Schlegel) Cave Salamander

1838 *Salamandra genei* Temminck & Schlegel
1926 *Hydromantes genei* Dunn

Until quite recently, two forms of this salamander found respectively in Sardinia and North Italy were regarded as separate species. The differences between the two are not, however, very great, and most authorities now agree that all the forms so far established—one in Sardinia and four on the mainland of Europe—should be regarded as related subspecies. Even this should be considered a tentative classification, since much still has to be learned about this secretive salamander, including the complete distribution, and little evidence of intergrading would be needed to offset some of the rather minor differences at present thought adequate to justify the mainland subspecies. On the other hand, the discovery of new populations could perhaps result in the establishment of further subspecies.

Throughout its range, the species is found only in mountainous regions, where it lives in damp conditions in rock crevices, under rocks, and in caves, or occasionally under logs or other debris.

Maximum size varies somewhat between the various forms, but in some areas can reach up to 4 in in the males and about $5\frac{1}{2}$ in in exceptionally large females. The mainland forms are generally slightly smaller than the Sardinian subspecies. The trunk is moderately slender and the limbs long. The head is flattened, almost hexagonal in plan, and behind the eyes is much broader than any part of the body. The short snout tapers rapidly in front of the eyes and is then strongly truncated and overhanging. The eyes are exceptionally large and prominent. Ten to thirteen vertical grooves are spaced out along each flank. The tail is almost completely cylindrical and not very long, making up less than half the total length. The four fingers are rather stubby and slightly webbed at the base, while the five toes are much longer and webbed for almost half their length. A prominent gular fold appears under the throat.

The tongue, as in other members of the genus, is quite a remarkable organ. It consists briefly of a large round disc mounted on a long stalk. Normally, the stalk is contained in a sheath running along the floor of the mouth, and has a highly corrugated surface. When required, the tongue can be protruded very rapidly and the concertina-like corrugations open as the stalk stretches to an amazing degree, allowing the tongue to be protruded some 10 to 12 mm. An excellent description of the mechanism involved is given by Elkan (1958).

The skin is very smooth with almost a polished appearance. No obvious sex differences present themselves except that breeding males develop a low oval-shaped swelling under the chin.

Colour varies quite considerably and will be described separately for each subspecies.

The species is entirely terrestrial and nocturnal. At night, particularly after rain, it may come out into the open and climb about among the rocks, being able to negotiate vertical surfaces with comparative ease.

Food consists mainly of small insects, arthropods, and myriapods, which are as it were 'aimed at' and picked up on the end of the rapidly protruded tongue. So far as is known, all food is caught in this manner and never seized in the jaws, which is probably the reason why more cumbersome creatures such as worms and slugs are apparently ignored.

Very little is known about the breeding habits of this secretive salamander. A form of courtship has been observed in which the male straddles the female, clasping her with his arms and legs in the neck and flanks. The chin gland is held against the top of the female's head and usually moved up to her snout, possibly as an aid to adjustment of position. Presumably a spermatophore is transferred, since fertilisation of the eggs is known to be internal, and the female gives birth to live young, some 35 to 40 mm long. Newly born young have been found at various times of the year, and it would seem that breeding is not confined to any particular season, though the highest proportion of births probably takes place in the spring.

HYDROMANTES GENEI GENEI (*TEMMINCK & SCHLEGEL*)

SARDINIAN CAVE SALAMANDER

1838 *Salamandra genei* Temminck & Schlegel

1925 *Hydromantes genei genei* Wolterstorff

This subspecies is fairly widely distributed in the more mountainous regions of Sardinia, particularly where caves and rocks provide suitable cover.

Apart from coloration, the differences between the various subspecies of the Cave Salamander are not very great, and the main morphological characteristics of this subspecies are the lack of a *canthus rostralis* (a depression running obliquely down each side of the snout), which is found in all other subspecies, and a tendency to grow slightly larger. The proportions of the limbs vary to some extent between the subspecies, though this is rarely an accurate guide to the identification of individual specimens; the subspecies *genei* has longer hind limbs than the others and the fingers of the hands are also longer.

The ground colour of the upper surface is usually dark brown, sometimes almost black and occasionally quite a light brown, with a mottled pattern of lighter markings. These markings are normally yellowish to reddish, but in some specimens may be greyish or greenish. The undersides are a fairly uniform light grey, often with a brownish and sometimes with almost a bluish tinge.

HYDROMANTES GENEI AMBROSII *LANZA*

SPEZIA CAVE SALAMANDER

1954 *Hydromantes italicus ambrosii* Lanza
1960 *Hydromantes genei ambrosii* Mertens & Wermuth

As far as is known, this form is found only in a small isolated area around Spezia, at the eastern end of the province of Liguria in north-west Italy.

The dorsal coloration is dark brown, and the undersides light grey—which on closer examination can be seen to consist of numerous white specks on a darker ground. The flanks and sides of the tail bear a number of blotches, varying in different individuals from nearly yellow to reddish brown, in some cases only feebly evident but sometimes prominent and numerous enough to give a general impression of an irregular coloured stripe.

HYDROMANTES GENEI GORMANI *LANZA*

CENTRAL CAVE SALAMANDER

1952 *Hydromantes italicus gormanii* Lanza
1960 *Hydromantes genei gormani* Mertens & Wermuth

The range of this species lies between that of *strinatii* to the west and *ambrosii* and *italicus* to the east. It is found in the mountainous areas of western Liguria and the extreme south of Piedmont, extending west as far as the eastern end of the Maritime Alps in south-east France.

There is a strong tendency for the yellowish to reddish-brown blotches to obscure the darker ground colour, by reason both of their intense colour and of their size, and sometimes parts or even the whole of the upper surface appears a lighter colour. The coloration of the undersides shows a similar tendency, in that the whitish specks run together to give a marbled effect or form fairly large blotches.

HYDROMANTES GENEI ITALICUS *DUNN*

EASTERN CAVE SALAMANDER

1923 *Hydromantes italicus* Dunn

1925 *Hydromantes genei italicus* Wolterstorff

Of the mainland species, this is the most important as regards both numbers and extent of range. It is found all along the main Italian mountain range which straddles almost the whole of the border between the provinces of Emilia and Tuscany; in addition, a number of what appear to be isolated populations occur both further east near the Adriatic coast, and continue along the central mountains of Italy as far south as the Abruzzi Mountains in Central Italy. It may well be that further populations have yet to be discovered.

The upper surface is dark brown, faintly spotted or blotched with lighter markings varying from pale red to light brown. These markings may be sparse and irregular, or more profuse to give the effect of marbling. The undersides are powdered with very small whitish specks, producing a general light-grey appearance.

HYDROMANTES GENEI STRINATII *AELLEN*

WESTERN CAVE SALAMANDER

1958 *Hydromantes italicus strinatii* Aellen

1960 *Hydromantes genei strinatii* Mertens & Wermuth

It will be seen from the above that the overall range of the mainland forms extends generally from Central Italy northwest along the main mountain range to skirt round the Gulf of Genoa into Liguria, and this population extends still further west into the more westerly parts of the Maritime Alps of south-east France. It was first described by Aellen from the Grotte d'Aspremont, and has subsequently been recorded from Mont Agel and Mont Leuze. Almost certainly, further recordings will extend its present rather limited known range.

It has certain resemblances to *gormani*, particularly as regards the coloration of the undersides, but more resembles *ambrosii* in the rather larger size of the hind limbs. In its dorsal coloration, however, it can readily be distinguished from both, the dark brown ground colour being relieved by a number of irregularly shaped light-brown blotches.

Page 143 (*above*) Northern Crested Newt *Triturus c. cristatus*. Female

(*below*) Palmate Newt *Triturus h. helveticus*. Female

CHAPTER 6

The Family Proteidae

As in the case of the plethodontids, we are dealing here with a family which has a fairly wide range in the New World and an isolated species in a comparatively small area in South Europe. It is, however, a much smaller family with only two genera, one in North America and one in Europe.

Apparently of considerable antiquity, its origins are unknown and it has no obvious relationship with any other family of urodeles. Its members are completely aquatic and neotenic, retaining the larval form as adults without undergoing metamorphosis. In this connection they retain a number of features found only in the larvae of other families, such as the formation and largely cartilaginous nature of the skullbones and the absence of eyelids. Moreover, although lungs of a sort are present, external gills are retained, except that the number of branchial arches has been reduced from four to three.

The American forms are largely found in surface waters such as rivers and streams, lakes and ponds, but the European species occurs only in underground waters, often at considerable depth. Fertilisation in all the species is internal by means of a spermatophore, which together with the general formation of the cloacal glands suggests perhaps a closer relationship with the salamandrids than with the hynobiids or cryptobranchids, but this is by no means certain.

GENUS *PROTEUS LAURENTI* 1768

Since only one species of this genus has been discovered, the diagnostic features will be given in the description of the species.

Proteus anguinus Laurenti 1768   **Olm**

The complete list of synonyms for this species is rather long and confusing, and will not be given in detail. It will perhaps suffice to say that it has been re-described more than once and attempts have been made to break it down into various species and subspecies subsequently regarded as invalid. Any references involving the generic names *Proteus, Hypochthon,* or *Phanerobranchus* apply to this species. An example is a form found in the area of Rupa near Schweinsdorf in Yugoslavia; this was first described by Fitzinger in 1850 as a separate species *Hypochthon zoisii,* later classified by Mertens & Müller (1940) as a subspecies of *Proteus anguinus,* but finally regarded by Mertens & Wermuth (1960) as synonymous with the typical form.

The species is found in underground lakes and streams in the limestone mountain areas ranging from the eastern end of the Alps in the province of Carinthia in extreme South Austria, south-east through Carniola and the neighbourhood of Trieste and along the western mountain ranges of Yugoslavia into Dalmatia and parts of Hercegovina. In some places it is found quite near the surface, in others much deeper, but the maximum depth to which it descends is not known. The temperature of these underground waters is fairly constant, varying little between summer and winter, and it is probable that in a wild state the Olm is rarely subjected to temperatures outside the range 5° to 10° C (41° to 50° F).

The extent to which this salamander is adapted to its particular habitat is reflected in its appearance. The head and body are elongated, giving an average total length in adults of 8 to 10 in and almost 12 in in exceptional cases. The snout is broadened, depressed, and truncated, apparently as an adaptation to burrowing in mud and fine sand, and the mouth is small. The eyes are rudimentary and do not reach the surface of the skin, though often indicated by a dark spot. Experiments suggest that they might retain a slight sensitivity to light, but for practical purposes the Olm can be regarded as blind. The long, cylindrical body has some two dozen or more weak costal grooves spaced along the whole length of each flank. The tail, strongly compressed laterally and forming a good swimming organ, is nevertheless not very long, making up little more than one third the total length and shorter than the body proper. It is fringed above and below with a smooth-edged cutaneous crest uniting around the extremity to make the latter bluntly rounded or at the most only feebly pointed. The limbs are small in proportion to the size of the body, with short stumpy toes, three on the front limbs and only two on the hind limbs. On each side of the neck, immediately behind the head, are three large tufted external gills.

The entire skin surface is dull white, though frequently with a pinkish tinge, and sometimes with a few dingy yellow or reddish dots and blotches. The gills, in contrast, are bright red. If exposed for a long enough period to light, the skin colour darkens, first to violet and eventually, over a few months, almost to uniform black. This process can be reversed if the animal is returned to the dark.

Sex differences are not immediately obvious but are apparent on closer examination, being largely confined to the formation of the cloacal region. This, in females, is furnished with a simple longitudinal slit, whereas in the males the slit bifurcates towards one end. The general shape of the cloacal protuberance also differs between the sexes, that of the male being larger anteriorly than posteriorly. The upper tail-fin in the male is slightly higher than that of the female, and develops low undulations during the breeding season. According to Chauvin (1883), two rows of light spots appear on the sides of the tail at the same time.

Food in the wild state appears to consist largely of a local fresh-water crustacean of the genus *Nyphargus*. In captivity, however, it has been found that small worms, tiny fish, and even shreds of raw meat are readily eaten.

No knowledge of breeding habits has been obtained from direct observation in the wild, as no eggs or larvae have been found. Observations in captivity have been confusing, as both egg-laying and birth of live young have occurred. It is now almost certain that the normal condition is for a number of eggs to start developing in the oviducts, but at some stage all the eggs bar one in each oviduct, or sometimes in one oviduct, break down to form a liquid which nourishes the remaining egg. This results in due course in the birth of one or two live young, about 4 in long. In water temperatures of more than about 12° to 13° C (around 55° F), this mechanism fails to function properly and all the eggs, which may number up to sixty, are laid as eggs. These either do not hatch or, if any of them do, the young are too small to survive. Newly born young have more fully developed eyes than the adults, but by the end of the first year the eyes have almost completely disappeared.

Distribution Maps

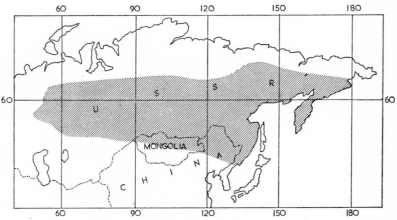

Map 1   Distribution of *Hynobius keyserlingi*

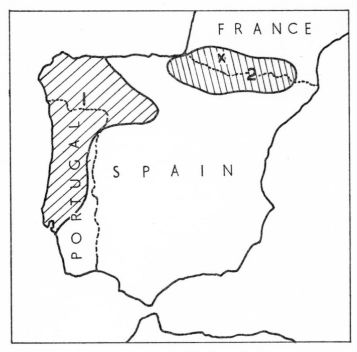

Map 2 Distribution of:
1 *Chioglossa lusitanica*
2 *Euproctus a. asper*
X *E. a. castelmouliensis*

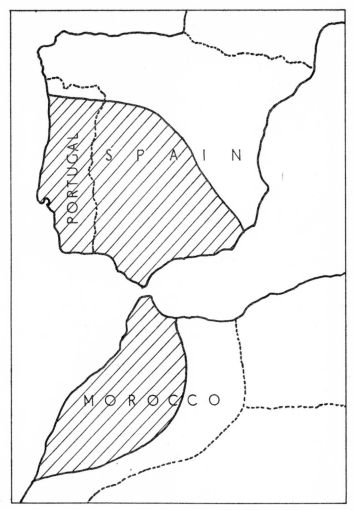

Map 3   Distribution of *Pleurodeles waltl*

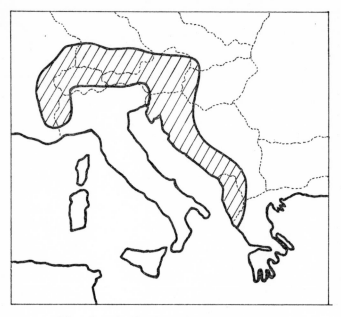

Map 4   Distribution of *Salamandra atra*

Map 5   Distribution of *Salamandra salamandra*

Subspecies: 1 *salamandra*   2 *almanzoris*   3 *bejarae*   4 *corsica*   5 *fastuosa*
6 *gallaica*   7 *gigliolii*   8 *terrestris*   9 *algira*   10 *semenovi*

Areas of interbreeding between subspecies are in places extensive, and to this extent the boundaries are schematic

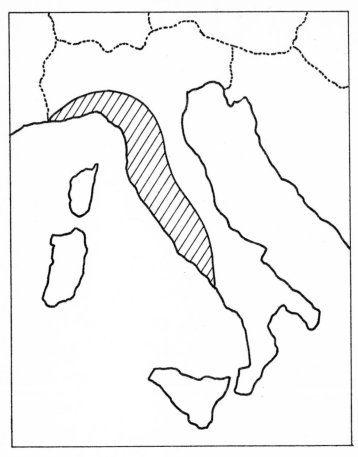

Map 6   Distribution of *Salamandrina terdigitata*

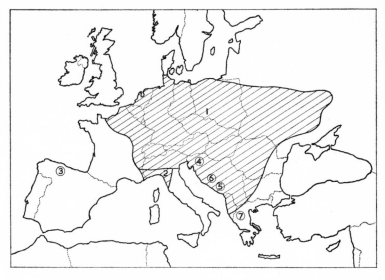

Map 7   Distribution of *Triturus alpestris*

Subspecies: 1 *alpestris*   5 *montenegrinus*
             2 *apuanas*   6 *reiseri*
             3 *cyreni*   7 *veluchiensis*
             4 *lacusnigri*

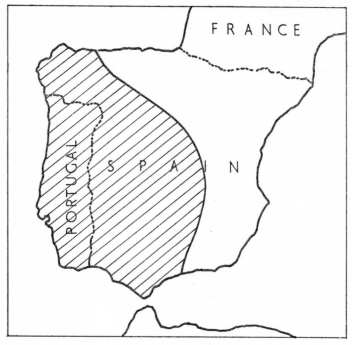

Map 8   Distribution of *Triturus boscai*

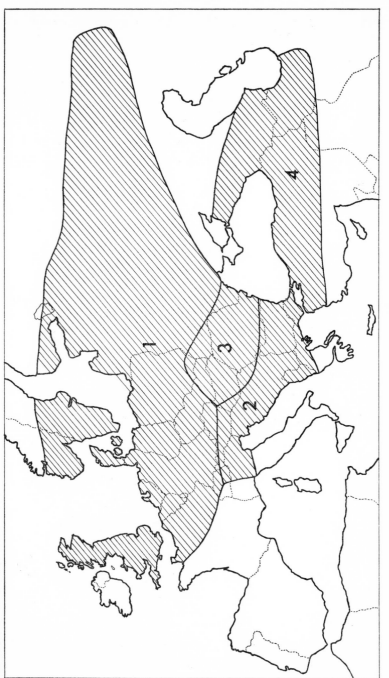

Map 9   Distribution of *Triturus cristatus*

Subspecies: 1 *cristatus*   2 *carnifex*   3 *dobrogicus*   4 *karelinii*

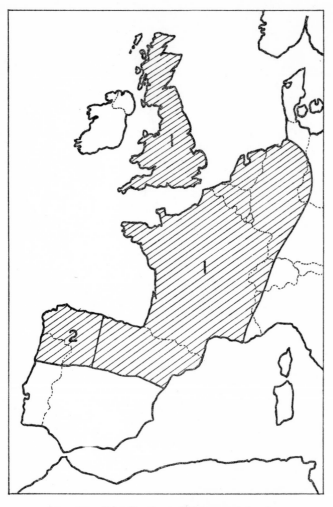

Map 10   Distribution of *Triturus helveticus*
Subspecies: 1   *helveticus*
             2   *sequeirai*

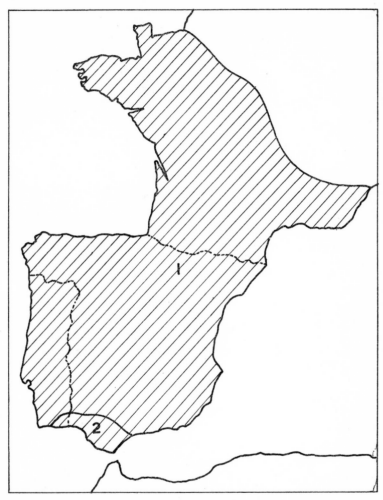

Map 11   Distribution of *Triturus marmoratus*
Subspecies :   1   *marmoratus*
　　　　　　　2   *pygmaeus*

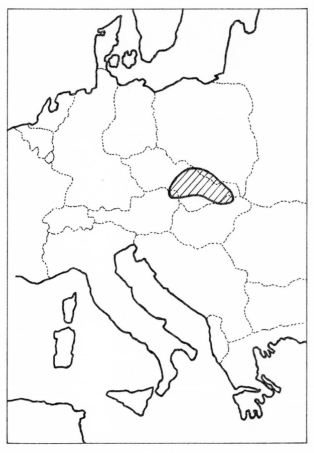

Map 12   Distribution of *Triturus montandoni*

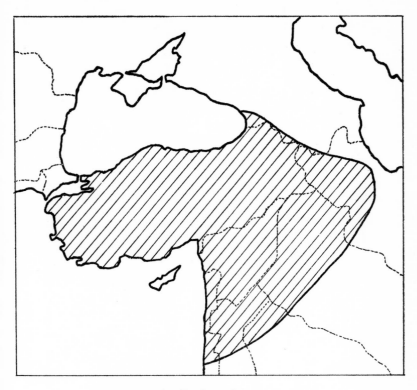

Map 13   Distribution of *Triturus vittatus*

K

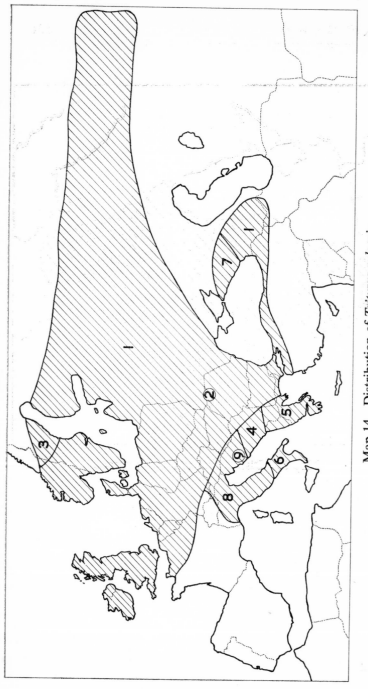

Map 14   Distribution of *Triturus vulgaris*

Subspecies: 1 *vulgaris*   2 *ampelensis*   3 *borealis*   4 *dalmaticus*   5 *graecus*
6 *italicus*   7 *lantzi*   8 *meridionalis*   9 *schreiberi*

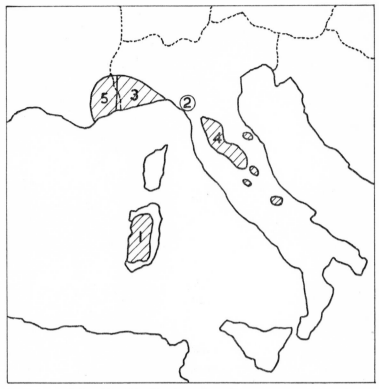

Map 15   Distribution of *Hydromantes genei*
Subspecies: 1 *genei*   4 *italicus*
              2 *ambrosii*   5 *strinatii*
              3 *gormani*

K*

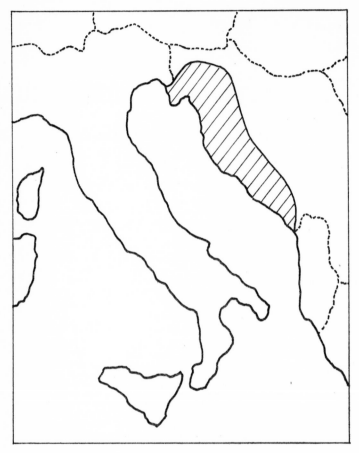

Map 16   Distribution of *Proteus anguinus*
The area shown covers places in which the species has
been found to date, but is necessarily speculative.
Further exploration of underground waters might prove
it to be too restricted

Common Names Used in European Countries

COMMON NAMES IN ENGLAND AND FRANCE

	English	*French*
Hynobius keyserlingi	Siberian Salamander	Salamandre de Sibérie
Salamandra salamandra	European Salamander	Salamandre terrestre
	Fire Salamander	Salamandre tachetée
Salamandra atra	Alpine Salamander	Salamandre alpestre
		Salamandre noire
Chioglossa lusitanica	Gold-striped Salamander	Chioglosse portugais
Euproctus asper	Pyrenean Mountain Salamander	Triton des Pyrénées
		Euprocte des Pyrénées
Euproctus montanus	Corsican Mountain Salamander	Triton de Corse
		Euprocte de Corse
Euproctus platycephalus	Sardinian Mountain Salamander	Triton de Sardaigne
	Flat-headed Salamander	Euprocte de Sardaigne
Pleurodeles waltl	Iberian Ribbed Newt	Triton d'Espagne
	(Spanish) Ribbed Newt	Triton à côtes
	Pleurodele Newt	Triton de Waltl
		Pleurodèle de Waltl
Salamandrina terdigitata	Spectacled Salamander	Salamandrine à lunettes
Triturus alpestris	Alpine Newt	Triton alpestre
Triturus boscai	Bosca's Newt	Triton de Bosca
Triturus cristatus	Crested Newt	Triton à crête
	(Great) Warty Newt	Triton crêté
Triturus helveticus	Palmate Newt	Triton palmé
Triturus marmoratus	Marbled Newt	Triton marbré
Triturus montandoni	Carpathian Newt	Triton de Montandon
	Montandon's Newt	
Triturus vittatus	Banded Newt	Triton à bandes
Triturus vulgaris	Smooth Newt	Triton ponctué
	Common Newt	Triton vulgaire
Hydromantes genei	(Brown) Cave Salamander	Spelerpe brun
		Hydromante

Proteus anguinus   Olm   Protée anguillard
                             Cave Salamander

COMMON NAMES IN GERMAN AND DUTCH

	German	*Dutch*
Hynobius keyserlingi	Sibirischer Winkelzahnmolch	
Salamandra salamandra	Feuer-salamander	Vuursalamander
Salamandra atra	Alpensalamander	Alpensalamander
Chioglossa lusitanica	Goldstreifen-Salamander	
Euproctus asper	Pyrenäen-Gebirgsmolch Rauhnolch	Pyreneeënsalamander
Euproctus montanus	Korsischer Gebirgsmolch	
Euproctus platycephalus	Hechtkopf-Gebirgsmolch	
Pleurodeles waltl	Spanischer Rippenmolch	
Salamandrina terdigitata	Brillensalamander	
Triturus alpestris	Bergmolch Alpenmolch	Alpenwatersalamander
Triturus boscai	Spanischer Wassermolch	Spaanse watersalamander
Triturus cristatus	Kammolch	Kamsalamander Grote watersalamander
Triturus helveticus	Fadenmolch Leistenmolch	Vinpootsalamander Draadstaartsalamander
Triturus marmoratus	Marmormolch	Marmersalamander
Triturus montandoni	Karpathenmolch	
Triturus vittatus	Bandmolch	
Triturus vulgaris	Teichmolch	Gewone watersalamander Kleine watersalamander
Hydromantes genei	Brauner Höhlensalamander Höhlenmolch	
Proteus anguinus	Grottenolm	

COMMON NAMES IN ITALIAN AND POLISH

	Italian	*Polish*
Salamandra salamandra	Salamandra comune Salamandra machiata	Salamandra plamista
Salamandra atra	Salamandra alpina	Salamandra czarna
Triturus alpestris	Tritone alpestre	Traszka gorska
Triturus cristatus	Tritone crestato	Traszka grzebieniasta
Triturus helveticus	Tritone palmato	
Triturus marmoratus	Tritone marmoreggiato	

Triturus montandoni	Tritone de Montandon	Traszka karpacka
Triturus vulgaris	Tritone comune	Traszka zwyczajna
	Tritone punteggiato	

COMMON NAMES IN CZECH AND RUSSIAN

	Czech	*Russian*
Hynobius keyserlingi		Сибирский углозуб
Salamandra salamandra	Mlok zemní	Пятнистая саламандра
Salamandra atra	Mlok černý	Альпийская саламандра
		Черная саламандра
Pleurodeles waltl		Иглистий тритон
Triturus alpestris	Čolek horský	Альпийский тритон
Triturus cristatus	Čolek velký	Гребенчатый тритон
Triturus montandoni	Čolek karpatský	Карпатский тритон
Triturus vittatus		Малоазиатский тритон
Triturus vulgaris	Čolek tečkovaný	Обыкновенный тритон
Proteus anguinus		Европейский протей

References and Bibliography

Aellen, V. *Senckenberg biol*, 39 (Frankfurt, 1958)

Ahrenfeldt, R. H. 'Mating behaviour of *Euproctus asper* in captivity', *Brit Journ Herpetol*, 2, 11 (London, 1960)

Angel, F. *Faune de France, Reptiles et Amphibiens* (Lechevalier, Paris, 1946)

Bedriaga, J. von. *Archiv für Naturgeschichte*, 49 (Berlin, 1883); *Inst Rev Sci Litt*, 2, 36 (Coimbra, 1889)

Bell, T. *A History of the British Reptiles* (Van Voorst, London, 1839)

Berthold. *Nachr könige Ges Wiss*, 12 (Göttingen, 1946)

Bocage, J. V. B. du. *Revue et Mag Zool*, 16 (Paris, 1864)

Bodenheimer, F. S. 'Introduction into the Knowledge of the Amphibia and Reptilia of Turkey', *Rev Fac Sci de L'Université d'Istanbul*, IX, 1 (Istanbul, 1944)

Bonaparte, L. *Iconografia della Fauna italica*, 2 (Rome, 1839)

Boulenger, G. A. *Bull Soc Zool France*, 5 (Paris, 1880); *Catalogue of the Batrachia Gradientia, s. Caudata and Batrachia Apoda in the collection of the British Museum* (London, 1882); *Les Batraciens et principalement ceux d'Europe* (Paris, 1910)

Bory, J. B. *Res Erpetol Hist Nat Rept* (1828)

Brooks, C. E. P. *Climate through the Ages* (revised ed), (Benn, London, 1949)

Bund, C. F. v.d. *Vierde Herpetogeografisch Verslag* (distribution of species in Holland), (Lacerta, Engelen, 1964)

Camerano, L. *Mem della Acad delle Scienze di Torino*, 2, 36 (Turin, 1885)

Chauvin, Marie von. 'Die Art der Fortpflanzung des *Proteus anguinus*', *Zeitschr Wiss Zool*, 38 (1883)

Cochran, D. M. *Living Amphibians of the World* (Hamilton, London, 1961)

Daudin, F. M. *Histoire naturelle, générale et particulière des reptiles*, 8 (Paris, 1803)

Duges, A. *Annales Sci Nat*, 3, 17 (Paris, 1852)

Dumeril, A. M. C. et Bibron, G. *Erpétologie générale, ou histoire naturelle complète des reptiles* (Paris, 1841)

Dunn, E. R. *Bull Mus comp Zool*, 62 (Cambridge, 1918); *Proc New England Zool Club*, 8 (Boston, 1923); *The Salamanders of the family Plethodontidae* (Northampton, Mass, 1926)

Dürigen, B. *Deutschlands Amphibien und Reptilien.* (Creutz'sche Verlag, Magdeburg, 1897)

Dybowski. *Beiträge zur Kenntnis der Wassermolche Sibiriens* (Vienna, 1870)

Eiselt. *Abh Berl Naturkunde Vorgesch Mus,* 10 (Magdeburg, 1958)

Elkan, E. 'The Cave Salamander' (*Hydromantes* Gistel), *Brit Journ Herpetol,* 2, 6 (London, 1958)

Fitter, R. S. R. *The Ark in our Midst* (Collins, London, 1959)

Fitzinger, L. J. *Neue Klassifikation der Reptilien* (Vienna, 1826); *Sber Akad Wiss Wien,* 5 (Vienna, 1850)

Ford, R. L. E. *British Reptiles and Amphibians* (Collins, London, 1954)

Frommhold, E. *Lurche und Kriechtiere Mitteleuropas* (Neumann, Radebeul, 1959)

Fuhn & Freytag. *Mitt Natur Vorgesch Museum,* 3 (Magdeburg, 1952)

Gadow, H. *Amphibia and Reptiles, Cambridge Natural History,* 8 (London, 1901)

Gené. *Mem Acad delle Scienze di Torino,* 2, 1 (Turin, 1838)

Gorman, J. 'Reproduction in plethodont salamanders of the genus *Hydromantes*', *Herpetologica,* 12, 4 (1956)

Gravenhorst, J. L. C. *Deliciae Musei Zoologici Vratislaviensis* (Leipzig, 1829)

Gray, J. E. *Catalogue of the specimens of Amphibia in the collection of the British Museum,* 2 (London, 1850)

Hellmich, W. *Die Lurche und Kriechtiere Europas* (Carl Winter, Heidelberg, 1956); (published in English 1962 as *Reptiles and Amphibians of Europe* by the Blandford Press, London)

Hillenius. 'De kweek van de Pyreneeensalamander (*Euproctus asper*)', Lacerta, 22, 1 (1963)

Hübener, H. 'Aziatische salamander in gevangenschap', *Lacerta,* 20, 6 (description of *Hynobius keyserlingi*), (1962)

Jenyns, L. *Manual of British vertebrate animals* (Cambridge, 1835).

Kauri, H. *Acta vertebr,* I (Stockholm, 1959)

Kiritzescu. *Bull Soc Sci,* 12 (Bucharest, 1903)

Kirtisinghe, P. *The Amphibia of Ceylon* (Colombo, 1957)

Kolombatović. *Glas narovosl Društva,* 19 (Zagreb, 1907)

Krassavzev, B. A. '*Hynobius keyserlingi* Dyb in Europe', *Zool Anzeiger,* XLIV, 5/8 (1931)

Lacépède, B. G. E. de. *Histoire naturelle des quadrupèdes ovipares et des serpents* (Paris, 1788)

Lanza. *Arch zool ital,* 39 (Naples, 1954)

Lataste, F. *Bulletin No 4 de la Soc Zool de France* (Paris, 1879)

Latreille, P. A. *Histoire naturelle des Salamandres de France* (Paris, 1800)

Lesson, R. P. *Revue Zoologique,* 2 (Paris, 1839)

Laurenti, J. N. *Synopsis reptilium* (Vienna, 1768)

Linnaeus, C. von. *Systema naturae,* Ed 10 (1758)

Litton, R. A. 'Leeches attacking Common Newt', *Brit Journ Herpetol,* 3 3 (London, 1962)

Loveridge, A. *Reptiles of the Pacific World* (Macmillan, London, 1946)

Mehely, L. von. *Ann hist nat Mus hungarici,* 3 (Budapest, 1905)

Meijer, R. M. 'Herpetologische belevenisse op Corsica', *Lacerta,* 21, 8 (reference to *Euproctus asper*), (1963)

Mertens, R. *Senckenbergiana,* 5 (Frankfurt, 1923); *Abh senckenb naturf Ges,*

41 (Frankfurt, 1925); *Welches Tier ist das?* *Kriechtiere und Lurche* (2nd ed), (Franckh'sche Verlag, Stuttgart, 1960); *The World of Amphibians and Reptiles* (Harrap, London, 1960)

Mertens, R. & Müller, L. *Abh senckenb naturf Ges*, 41 (Frankfurt, 1928); 'Die Amphibien und Reptilien Europas (Zweite Liste)', *Abh senckenb naturf Ges*, 451 (Frankfurt, 1940)

Mertens, R. & Wermuth, H. *Die Amphibien und Reptilien Europas* (Dritte Liste), (Kramer, Frankfurt, 1960)

Michahelles. 'Neue südeuropäische Amphibien', *Isis*, 23 (Leipzig, 1830)

Müller, L. & Hellmich, W. *Zool Anz*, 112 (Leipzig, 1935).

Nazarov, A. A. 'Sibirskiy uglozub b Evrope', *Priroda*, 22 (1968)

Nikolskiy, A. M. *Fauna Rossiy Akademia Nauk* (Moscow, 1918)

Noble, G. K. *The Biology of the Amphibia* (Dover Publications, London, 1931)

Olexa, A. & Kral, J. 'Uber Fang, Transport und Haltung des Bandmolches *Triturus vittatus*', *Aquarien-Terrarien*, 10, 4 (1963)

Pasteur, G. & Bons, J. 'Les Batraciens du Maroc', *Travaux de l'Inst Sci Cherifien, Serie Zool*, 17 (Rabat, 1959)

Peracca, M. G. *Boll Mus Zool Torino*, 13 (Turin, 1898)

Poche, F. *Verh zool-botan Ges*, 61 (Vienna, 1911)

Radovanovic. *Vodozemci i gmizavci naše zemlje* (1951)

Razoumowsky. *Histoire naturele du Jurat*, 1 (Lausanne, 1789)

Rensch, B. *Evolution above the species level* (London, 1959)

Salthe, S. N. 'Courtship Patterns and the Phylogeny of the Urodeles', *Copeia* 1967, No 1 (Washington, 1967)

Savi, P. *Giorn Lett Sci Art*, 22 (Milan, 1821)

Schneider, J. C. *Historiae Amphibiorum naturalis et literariae*, 1 (Jena, 1799)

Schreiber, E. *Herpetologia Europaea* (Fischer, Jena, 1912)

Seliškar, A. & Pehani. *Verh internat Ver Limnol*, 7 (Stuttgart, 1935)

Smith, Malcolm. *The British Amphibians and Reptiles* (revised ed), (Collins, London, 1954).

Steward, J. W. 'Resort to water outside the breeding season of the Crested Newt *Triturus c. cristatus* (Laurenti)', *Brit Journ Herpetol*, 3, 11 (London, 1966)

Stirton, R. A. *Time, Life and Man* (Chapman & Hall, London, 1959)

Strauch, A. 'Revision der Salamandriden-Gattungen', *Mem Acad St Petersbourg*, 16 (1870)

Syroechkovskiy, E. E. 'Zagadka uglozuba', *Vokrug Sbeta*, 9 (1966)

Temminck, C. J. & Schlegel, H. in Siebold, Temminck & Schlegel: *Fauna Japonica, Reptilia* (Leyden, 1838)

Terentyev, P. V. *Herpetologia* (Moscow, 1961)

Terentyev, P. V. & Chernov, S. A. *Kratkiy opredelitel zemnovodnykh i presmykayushchikhsya S.S.S.R.* (Sovietskaya Nauka, Moscow, 1936); *Opredelitel presmykayushchikhsya i zemnovodnykh* (Sovietskaya Nauka, Moscow, 1949)

Termier, H. & G. *The Geological Drama* (Hutchinson, London, 1958)

Thorn, R. 'Protection of the brood by the male of the salamander *Hynobius nebulosus*', *Copeia* 1963, 3 (Northridge, California, 1962); 'Contribution a l'étude d'une salamandre japonaise, L'*Hynobius nebulosus* (Schlegel). Comportement et reproduction en captivité', *Inst Grand-Ducal de Luxembourg, Section des Sciences, Archives*, 22 (Luxemburg, 1963);

'Nouvelles observations sur l'éthologie sexuelle de l'*Hynobius nebulosus* (Temminck et Schlegel) (Caudata, Hynobiidae)', *Inst Grand-Ducal de Luxembourg, Section des Sciences naturelles*, Vol XXXII (Luxemburg, 1967)

Tschudi, J. T. 'Classification der Batrachier mit Berücksichtigung der fossilen Thiere dieser Abteilung der Reptilien', *Mem Soc Sci nat Neuchatel*, 2 (1838)

Turyeva, V. V. 'O nakhozhdeniy sibirskovo chetyrekhpalovo tritona b Komi A.S.S.R.', *Priroda*, 8 (1948)

Werner, F. *Verh zool-botan Ges*, 52 (Vienna, 1902)

Wolterstorff, W. (1) *Congr internat Zool Berne*, 6; (2) *Zool Anzeiger*, 29 (Leipzig, 1905); *Aquarien- und Terrarienkunde*, 5 (Magdeburg, 1908); *Abh Ber Mus*, 2 (Magdeburg, 1914); *Aquarien- und Terrarienkunde*, 34 (Stuttgart, 1923); *Abh Ber Mus*, 4 (Magdeburg, 1925); *Zool Anzeiger*, 97 (Leipzig, 1932); *Aquarien- und Terrarienkunde*, 45 (Stuttgart, 1934); *Aquarien- und Terrarienkunde*, 46 (Stuttgart, 1935)

Wooldridge, S. W. & Morgan, R. S. *An Outline of Geomorphology* (2nd ed), (Longmans Green, London, 1959)

Woollacott, A. 'Notes on the distribution and ecology of reptiles and amphibians in the Eyrewash Valley area of Nottinghamshire and Derbyshire', *Brit Journ Herpetol*, 3, 4 (London, 1963)

Zeuner, F. E. *Dating the Past* (4th ed), (Methuen, London, 1958)

Acknowledgments

ACKNOWLEDGMENTS to the cynical must sometimes appear to be a defence against possible charges of plagiarism. To the extent that I have drawn upon published material, I admit the plagiarism, though I have done my best to ensure that it was justified. As far as possible, information obtained from published material is covered by references in the text and the original publications listed in the section 'References and Bibliography'. Similar references are included where I have touched upon some subject which a few readers at least might wish to read up in greater detail. Material not previously published in this country has been made available from many sources, as have both live and preserved specimens of a number of species and subspecies which I might otherwise have had difficulty in obtaining. For the valuable assistance given in this way, I would particularly like to thank Grahame Dangerfield (who also took most of the photographs), Dr Guenther Peters of the Zoological Museum in East Berlin, Prof P. V. Terentyev of the Zoological Museum in Leningrad, and Robert Thorn of Luxemburg, as well as the many members of the British Herpetological Society who have taken an interest in this publication.

Index to Species References

(Page numbers in bold type indicate main descriptive sections)

COMMON NAMES

SCIENTIFIC NAMES